TensorFlow: Powerful Predictive Analytics with TensorFlow

A fast-paced guide on supervised, unsupervised, and reinforcement learning with TensorFlow

Md. Rezaul Karim

BIRMINGHAM - MUMBAI

TensorFlow: Powerful Predictive Analytics with TensorFlow

First published: March 2018

Production reference: 1080318

Published by Packt Publishing Ltd.

Livery Place, 35 Livery Street

Birmingham B3 2PB, UK.

ISBN 978-1-78913-691-3

www.packtpub.com

Credits

This book is a blend of text and quizzes, all packaged up keeping your journey in mind. It includes content from the following Packt product:

- *Predictive Analytics with TensorFlow* by *Md. Rezaul Karim*

Meet Your Expert

We have the best work of the following esteemed author to ensure that your learning journey is smooth:

Md. Rezaul Karim has more than 8 years of experience in the area of research and development with a solid knowledge of algorithms and data structures in C/C++, Java, Scala, R, and Python focusing big data technologies: Spark, Kafka, DC/OS, Docker, Mesos, Zeppelin, Hadoop, and MapReduce and deep learning technologies: TensorFlow, DeepLearning4j, and H2O-Sparking Water. His research interests include machine learning, deep learning, semantic web/linked data, big data, and bioinformatics. He is a research scientist at Fraunhofer FIT, Germany. He is also a Ph.D. candidate at the RWTH Aachen University, Aachen, Germany. He holds a BSc and an MSc degree in computer science. Before joining the Fraunhofer FIT, he had been working as a researcher at Insight Centre for Data Analytics, Ireland. Before that, he worked as a lead engineer with Samsung Electronics' distributed R&D Institutes in Korea, India, Vietnam, Turkey, and Bangladesh. Before that, he worked as a research assistant in the Database Lab at Kyung Hee University, Korea. He also worked as an R&D engineer with BMTech21 Worldwide, Korea. Even before that, he worked as a software engineer with i2SoftTechnology, Dhaka, Bangladesh. He is the author of the following book titles with Packt Publishing:

- *Large-Scale Machine Learning with Spark*
- *Deep Learning with TensorFlow*
- *Scala and Spark for Big Data Analytics*
- *Predictive Analytics with TensorFlow*

Table of Contents

Preface

Predictive analytics discovers hidden patterns from structured and unstructured data for automated decision making in business intelligence. Predictive decisions are becoming a huge trend worldwide, catering to wide industry sectors by predicting which decisions are more likely to give maximum results. Data mining, statistics, and machine learning allow users to discover predictive intelligence by uncovering patterns and showing the relationship between structured and unstructured data.

Machine learning is concerned with algorithms that transform raw data into information and then into actionable intelligence. This fact makes machine learning well suited to the predictive analytics. Without machine learning, therefore, it would be nearly impossible to keep up with these massive streams of information altogether.

What's in It for Me?

Maps are vital for your journey, especially when you're holidaying in another continent. When it comes to learning, a roadmap helps you in giving a definitive path for progressing towards the goal. So, here you're presented with a roadmap before you begin your journey.

This book is meticulously designed and developed in order to empower you with all the right and relevant information on TensorFlow. We've created this Learning Path for you that consists of four lessons:

Lesson 1, From Data to Decisions – Getting Started with TensorFlow, provides a detailed description of the main TensorFlow features in a real-life problem, followed by detailed discussions about TensorFlow installation and configuration. It then covers computation graphs, data, and programming models before getting started with TensorFlow. The last part of the lesson contains an example of implementing linear regression model for predictive analytics.

Lesson 2, Putting Data in Place – Supervised Learning for Predictive Analytics, covers some TensorFlow-based supervised learning techniques from a theoretical and practical perspective. In particular, the linear regression model for regression analysis will be covered on a real dataset. It then shows how you could solve the Titanic survival problem using logistic regression, random forests, and SVMs for predictive analytics.

Lesson 3, Clustering Your Data – Unsupervised Learning for Predictive Analytics, digs deeper into predictive analytics and finds out how you can take advantage of it to cluster records belonging to the certain group or class for a dataset of unsupervised observations. It will then provide some practical examples of unsupervised learning. Particularly, clustering techniques using TensorFlow will be discussed with some hands-on examples.

Lesson 4, Using Reinforcement Learning for Predictive Analytics, talks about designing machine learning systems driven by criticism and rewards. It will show several examples on how to apply reinforcement learning algorithms for developing predictive models on real-life datasets.

What Will I Get From This Book?

- Learn TensorFlow features in a real-life problem, followed by detailed TensorFlow installation and configuration
- Explore computation graphs, data, and programming models also get an insight to an example of implementing linear regression model for predictive analytics
- Solve the Titanic survival problem using logistic regression, random forests, and SVMs for predictive analytics
- Dig deeper into predictive analytics and find out how to take advantage of it to cluster records belonging to the certain group or class for a dataset of unsupervised observations
- Learn several examples of how to apply reinforcement learning algorithms for developing predictive models on real-life datasets

Prerequisites

This book is aimed at data analysts, data scientists, and machine learning practitioners who want to build powerful, robust, and accurate predictive models with the power of TensorFlow. Some of the prerequisites that is required before you begin this book are:

- Working knowledge of Python
- Basic knowledge of TensorFlow
- Basic knowledge of Math and Statistics

1
From Data to Decisions – Getting Started with TensorFlow

Despite the huge availability of data and significant investments, many business organizations still go on gut feel because they neither make the proper use of the data nor do they take appropriate and effective business decisions. TensorFlow, on the other hand, can be used to help take the business decision from this huge collection of data. TensorFlow is mathematical software and an open source software library for Machine Intelligence, developed in 2011 by the Google Brain Team and it can be used to help us analyze data to predict the effective business outcome. Although the initial target of TensorFlow was to conduct research in machine learning and in deep neural networks, however, the system is general enough to be applicable in a wide variety of other domains as well.

Keeping in mind your needs and based on all the latest and exciting features of TensorFlow 1.x, in this lesson, we will give a description of the main TensorFlow capabilities that are mostly motivated by a real-life example using the data.

The following topics will be covered in this lesson:

- From data to decision: Titanic example
- General overview of TensorFlow
- Installing and configuring TensorFlow
- TensorFlow computational graph
- TensorFlow programming model
- TensorFlow data model

- Visualizing through TensorBoard
- Getting started with TensorFlow: linear regression and beyond

Taking Decisions Based on Data – Titanic Example

The growing demand for data is a key challenge. Decision support teams such as institutional research and business intelligence often cannot take the right decisions on how to expand their business and research outcomes from a huge collection of data. Although data plays an important role in driving the decision, however, in reality, taking the right decision at right time is the goal.

In other words, the goal is the decision support, not the data support. This can be achieved through an advanced use of data management and analytics.

Data Value Chain for Making Decisions

The following diagram in figure 1 (source: *H. Gilbert Miller and Peter Mork, From Data to Decisions: A Value Chain for Big Data, Proc. Of IT Professional, Volume: 15, Issue: 1, Jan.-Feb. 2013, DOI: 10.1109/MITP.2013.11*) shows the data chain towards taking actual decisions–that is, the goal. The value chains start through the data discovery stage consisting of several steps such as data collection and annotating data preparation, and then organizing them in a logical order having the desired flow. Then comes the data integration for establishing a common data representation of the data. Since the target is to take the right decision, for future reference having the appropriate provenance of the data–that is, where it comes from, is important:

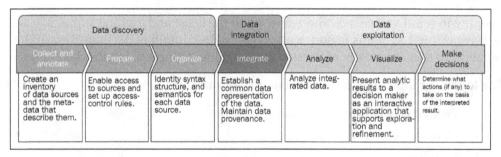

Figure 1: From data to decisions: a value chain for big data

Well, now your data is somehow integrated into a presentable format, it's time for the data exploration stage, which consists of several steps such as analyzing the integrated data and visualization before taking the actions to take on the basis of the interpreted results.

However, is this enough before taking the right decision? Probably not! The reason is that it lacks enough analytics, which eventually helps to take the decision with an actionable insight. Predictive analytics comes in here to fill the gap between. Now let's see an example of how in the following section.

From Disaster to Decision – Titanic Survival Example

Here is the challenge, Titanic–Machine Learning from Disaster from Kaggle (https://www.kaggle.com/c/titanic):

"The sinking of the RMS Titanic is one of the most infamous shipwrecks in history. On April 15, 1912, during her maiden voyage, the Titanic sank after colliding with an iceberg, killing 1502 out of 2224 passengers and crew. This sensational tragedy shocked the international community and led to better safety regulations for ships. One of the reasons that the shipwreck led to such loss of life was that there were not enough lifeboats for the passengers and crew. Although there was some element of luck involved in surviving the sinking, some groups of people were more likely to survive than others, such as women, children, and the upper-class. In this challenge, we ask you to complete the analysis of what sorts of people were likely to survive. In particular, we ask you to apply the tools of machine learning to predict which passengers survived the tragedy."

But going into this deeper, we need to know about the data of passengers travelling in the Titanic during the disaster so that we can develop a predictive model that can be used for survival analysis.

The dataset can be downloaded from the preceding URL. Table 1 here shows the metadata about the Titanic survival dataset:

Variable	Definition
survival	Two labels: 0 = No 1 = Yes
pclass	This is a proxy for the **Socioeconomic Status** (SES) of a passenger that is categorized as upper, middle and lower. In particular, 1 = 1st, 2 = 2nd, 3 = 3rd
sex	Male or female
Age	Age in years
sibsp	This signifies the family relation as follows: Sibling = brother, sister, stepbrother, stepsister Spouse = husband, wife (mistresses and fiancés were ignored)
parch	In the dataset, family relations are defined as follows: Parent = mother, father Child = daughter, son, stepdaughter, stepson Some children travelled only with a nanny, therefore parch=0 for them
ticket	Ticket number
fare	Passenger ticket fare
cabin	Cabin number
embarked	Three ports: C = Cherbourg Q = Queenstown S = Southampton

A snapshot of the dataset can be seen as follows:

PassengerId	Survived	Pclass	Name	Sex	Age	SibSp	Parch	Ticket	Fare	Cabin	Embarked
1	0	3	Braund, Mr. Owen Harris	male	22	1	0	A/5 21171	7.25		S
2	1	1	Cumings, Mrs. John Bradley (Florence Briggs Thayer)	female	38	1	0	PC 17599	71.2833	C85	C
3	1	3	Heikkinen, Miss. Laina	female	26	0	0	STON/O2. 3101282	7.925		S
4	1	1	Futrelle, Mrs. Jacques Heath (Lily May Peel)	female	35	1	0	113803	53.1	C123	S
5	0	3	Allen, Mr. William Henry	male	35	0	0	373450	8.05		S
6	0	3	Moran, Mr. James	male		0	0	330877	8.4583		Q
7	0	1	McCarthy, Mr. Timothy J	male	54	0	0	17463	51.8625	E46	S
8	0	3	Palsson, Master. Gosta Leonard	male	2	3	1	349909	21.075		S
9	1	3	Johnson, Mrs. Oscar W (Elisabeth Vilhelmina Berg)	female	27	0	2	347742	11.1333		S
10	1	2	Nasser, Mrs. Nicholas (Adele Achem)	female	14	1	0	237736	30.0708		C
11	1	3	Sandstrom, Miss. Marguerite Rut	female	4	1	1	PP 9549	16.7	G6	S
12	1	1	Bonnell, Miss. Elizabeth	female	58	0	0	113783	26.55	C103	S
13	0	3	Saundercock, Mr. William Henry	male	20	0	0	A/5. 2151	8.05		S
14	0	3	Andersson, Mr. Anders Johan	male	39	1	5	347082	31.275		S
15	0	3	Vestrom, Miss. Hulda Amanda Adolfina	female	14	0	0	350406	7.8542		S

Figure 2: A snapshot of the Titanic survival dataset

The ultimate target of using this dataset is to predict what kind of people survived the Titanic disaster. However, a bit of exploratory analysis of the dataset is a mandate. At first, we need to import necessary packages and libraries:

```
import pandas as pd
import matplotlib.pyplot as plt
import numpy as np
```

Now read the dataset and create a panda's DataFrame:

```
df = pd.read_csv('/home/asif/titanic_data.csv')
```

Before drawing the distribution of the dataset, let's specify the parameters for the graph:

```
fig = plt.figure(figsize=(18,6), dpi=1600)
alpha=alpha_scatterplot = 0.2
alpha_bar_chart = 0.55
fig = plt.figure()
ax = fig.add_subplot(111)
```

Draw a bar diagram for showing who survived versus who did not:

```
ax1 = plt.subplot2grid((2,3),(0,0))
ax1.set_xlim(-1, 2)
df.Survived.value_counts().plot(kind='bar', alpha=alpha_bar_chart)
plt.title("Survival distribution: 1 = survived")
```

Plot a graph showing survival by Age:

```
plt.subplot2grid((2,3),(0,1))
plt.scatter(df.Survived, df.Age, alpha=alpha_scatterplot)
plt.ylabel("Age")
plt.grid(b=True, which='major', axis='y')
plt.title("Survival by Age: 1 = survived")
```

Plot a graph showing distribution of the passengers classes:

```
ax3 = plt.subplot2grid((2,3),(0,2))
df.Pclass.value_counts().plot(kind="barh", alpha=alpha_bar_chart)
ax3.set_ylim(-1, len(df.Pclass.value_counts()))
plt.title("Class dist. of the passengers")
```

Plot a kernel density estimate of the subset of the 1st class passengers' age:

```
plt.subplot2grid((2,3),(1,0), colspan=2)
df.Age[df.Pclass == 1].plot(kind='kde')
df.Age[df.Pclass == 2].plot(kind='kde')
df.Age[df.Pclass == 3].plot(kind='kde')
plt.xlabel("Age")
plt.title("Age dist. within class")
plt.legend(('1st Class', '2nd Class','3rd Class'),loc='best')
```

Plot a graph showing `passengers per boarding location`:

```
ax5 = plt.subplot2grid((2,3),(1,2))
df.Embarked.value_counts().plot(kind='bar', alpha=alpha_bar_chart)
ax5.set_xlim(-1, len(df.Embarked.value_counts()))
plt.title("Passengers per boarding location")
Finally, we show all the subplots together:
plt.show()
>>>
```

The figure shows the survival distribution, survival by age, age distribution, and the passengers per boarding location:

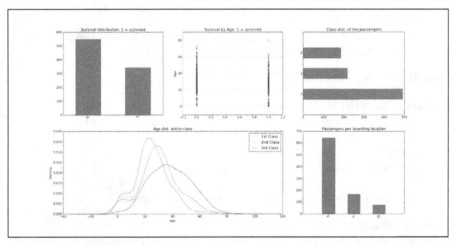

Figure 3: Titanic survival data distribution across age, class, and age within classes and boarding location

However, to execute the preceding code, you need to install several packages such as matplotlib, pandas, and scipy. They are listed as follows:

- **Installing pandas**: Pandas is a Python package for data manipulation. It can be installed as follows:

```
$ sudo pip3 install pandas

#For Python 2.7, use the following:

$ sudo pip install pandas
```

- **Installing matplotlib**: In the preceding code, matplotlib is a plotting library for mathematical objects. It can be installed as follows:

```
$ sudo apt-get install python-matplotlib    # for Python 2.7
$ sudo apt-get install python3-matplotlib # for Python 3.x
```

- **Installing scipy**: Scipy is a Python package for scientific computing. Installing blas and lapackand gfortran are a prerequisite for this one. Now just execute the following command on your terminal:

```
$ sudo apt-get install libblas-dev liblapack-dev $ sudo apt-get
install gfortran $ sudo pip3 install scipy # for Python 3.x

$ sudo pip install scipy # for Python 2.7
```

For Mac, use the following command to install the above modules:

```
$ sudo easy_install pip
$ sudo pip install matplotlib
$ sudo pip install libblas-dev liblapack-dev
$ sudo pip install gfortran
$ sudo pip install scipy
```

For windows, I am assuming that Python 2.7 is already installed at C:\Python27. Then open the command prompt and type the following command:

```
C:\Users\admin-karim>cd C:/Python27

C:\Python27> python -m pip install <package_name> # provide package name
accordingly.
```

For Python3, issue the following commands:

```
C:\Users\admin-karim>cd C:\Users\admin-karim\AppData\Local\Programs\
Python\Python35\Scripts

C:\Users\admin-karim\AppData\Local\Programs\Python\Python35\
Scripts>python3 -m pip install <package_name>
```

Well, we have seen the data. Now it's your turn to do some analytics on top of the data. Say predicting what kinds of people survived from that disaster. Don't you agree that we have enough information about the passengers, but how could we do the predictive modeling so that we can draw some fairly straightforward conclusions from this data?

For example, say being a woman, being in 1st class, and being a child were all factors that could boost passenger chances of survival during this disaster.

In a brute-force approach–for example, using if/else statements with some sort of weighted scoring system, you could write a program to predict whether a given passenger would survive the disaster. However, does writing such a program in Python make much sense? Naturally, it would be very tedious to write, difficult to generalize, and would require extensive fine tuning for each variable and samples (that is, passenger).

This is where predictive analytics with machine learning algorithms and emerging tools comes in so that you could build a program that learns from the sample data to predict whether a given passenger would survive. In such cases, we will see throughout this book that TensorFlow could be a perfect solution to achieve outstanding accuracies across your predictive models. We will start describing the general overview of the TensorFlow framework. Then we will show how to install and configure TensorFlow on Linux, Mac OS and Windows.

General Overview of TensorFlow

TensorFlow is an open source framework from Google for scientific and numerical computation based on dataflow graphs that stand for the TensorFlow's execution model. The dataflow graphs used in TensorFlow help the machine learning experts to perform more advanced and intensive training on the data for developing deep learning and predictive analytics models. In 2015, Google open sourced the TensorFlow and all of its reference implementation and made all the source code available on GitHub under the Apache 2.0 license. Since then, TensorFlow has achieved wide adoption from academia and research to the industry, and following that recently the most stable version 1.x has been released with a unified API.

As the name TensorFlow implies, operations are performed by neural networks on multidimensional data arrays (aka flow of tensors). This way, TensorFlow provides some widely used and robust implementation linear models and deep learning algorithms.

Deploying a predictive or general purpose model using TensorFlow is pretty straightforward. The thing is that once you have constructed your neural networks model after necessary feature engineering, you can simply perform the training interactively using plotting or TensorBoard (we will see more on it in upcoming sections). Finally, you deploy it eventually after evaluating it by feeding it some test data.

Since we are talking about the dataflow graphs, nodes in a flow graph correspond to the mathematical operations, such as addition, multiplication, matrix factorization, and so on, whereas, edges correspond to tensors that ensure communication between edges and nodes, that is dataflow and controlflow.

You can perform the numerical computation on a CPU. Nevertheless, using TensorFlow, it is also possible to distribute the training across multiple devices on the same system and train on them, especially if you have more than one GPU on your system so that these can share the computational load. But the precondition is if TensorFlow can access these devices, it will automatically distribute the computations to the multiple devices via a greedy process. But TensorFlow also allows the program, to specify which operations will be on which devices via name scope placement.

The APIs in TensorFlow 1.x have changed in ways that are not all backward compatible. That is, TensorFlow programs that worked on TensorFlow 0.x won't necessarily work on TensorFlow 1.x.

The main features offered by the latest release of TensorFlow are:

- **Faster computing**: The latest release of TensorFlow is incredibly faster. For example, it is 7.3 times faster on 8 GPUs for Inception v3 and 58 times speedup for distributed inception (v3 training on 64 GPUs).

- **Flexibility**: TensorFlow is not just a deep learning library, but it comes with almost everything you need for powerful mathematical operations through functions for solving the most difficult problems. TensorFlow 1.x introduces some high-level APIs for high-dimensional arrays or tensors, with `tf.layers`, `tf.metrics`, `tf.losses`, and `tf.keras` modules. These have made TensorFlow very suitable for high-level neural networks computing.

- **Portability**: TensorFlow runs on Windows, Linux, and Mac machines and on mobile computing platforms (that is, Android).

- **Easy debugging**: TensorFlow provides the TensorBoard tool for the analysis of the developed models.

- **Unified API**: TensorFlow offers you a very flexible architecture that enables you to deploy computation to one or more CPUs or GPUs in a desktop, server, or mobile device with a single API.

- **Transparent use of GPU computing**: Automating management and optimization of the same memory and the data used. You can now use your machine for large-scale and data-intensive GPU computing with NVIDIA cuDNN and CUDA toolkits.

- **Easy use**: TensorFlow is for everyone, it's for students, researchers, deep learning practitioners, and also for readers of this book.

- **Production ready at scale**: Recently it has evolved as the neural network for machine translation, at production scale. TensorFlow 1.x promises Python API stability, making it easier to choose new features without worrying too much about breaking your existing code.

- **Extensibility**: TensorFlow is relatively newer technology and it's still under active development. However, it is extensible because it was released with source code available on GitHub (`https://github.com/tensorflow/tensorflow`).

- **Supported**: There is a large community of developers and users working together to make TensorFlow a better product, both by providing feedback and by actively contributing to the source code.

- **Wide adoption**: Numerous tech giants are using TensorFlow for increasing their business intelligence. For example, ARM, Google, Intel, eBay, Qualcomm, SAM, Drobox, DeepMind, Airbnb, Twitter, and so on.

Throughout the next lesson, we will see how to achieve these features for predictive analytics.

Installing and Configuring TensorFlow

You can install and use TensorFlow on a number of platforms such as Linux, Mac OS, and Windows. Moreover, you can also build and install TensorFlow from the latest GitHub source of TensorFlow. Furthermore, if you have a Windows machine, you can install TensorFlow via native pip or Anacondas. It is to be noted that TensorFlow supports Python 3.5.x and 3.6.x on Windows.

Also, Python 3 comes with the pip3 package manager, which is the program you'll use to install TensorFlow. So you don't need to install pip if you're using this Python version. For simplicity, in this section, I will show you how to install TensorFlow using native pip. Now to install TensorFlow, start a terminal. Then issue the appropriate `pip3 install` command in that terminal.

To install the CPU-only version of TensorFlow, enter the following command:

```
C:\> pip3 install --upgrade tensorflow
```

To install the GPU version of TensorFlow, enter the following command:

```
C:\> pip3 install --upgrade tensorflow-gpu
```

When it comes to Linux, the TensorFlow Python API supports Python 2.7 and Python 3.3+, so you need to install Python to start the TensorFlow installation. You must install Cuda Toolkit 7.5 and cuDNN v5.1+ to get the GPU support. In this section, we will show you how to install and get started with TensorFlow. More details on installing TensorFlow on Linux will be shown.

> Installing on Mac OS is more or less similar to Linux. Please refer to the https://www.tensorflow.org/install/install_mac for more details. On the other hand, Windows users should refer to https://www.tensorflow.org/install/install_windows.

Note that for this and the rest of the lesson, we will provide most of the source codes with Python 3.x compatible.

Installing TensorFlow on Linux

In this section, we will show you how to install TensorFlow on Ubuntu 14.04 or higher. The instructions presented here also might be applicable for other Linux distributions with minimal adjustments.

However, before proceeding with formal steps, we need to determine which TensorFlow to install on your platform. TensorFlow has been developed such that you can run data intensive tensor applications on a GPU as well as a CPU. Thus, you should choose one of the following types of TensorFlow to install on your platform:

- **TensorFlow with CPU support only**: If there is no GPU such as NVIDIA® installed on your machine, you must install and start computing using this version. This is very easy and you can do it in just 5 to 10 minutes.

- **TensorFlow with GPU support**: As you might know, a deep learning application requires typically very high intensive computing resources. Thus TensorFlow is no exception, but can typically speed up the data computation and analytics significantly faster on a GPU rather than on a CPU. Therefore, if there's NVIDIA® GPU hardware on your machine, you should ultimately install and use this version.

From our experience, even if you have NVIDIA GPU hardware integrated on your machine, it would be worth installing and trying the CPU-only version first and if you don't experience good performance you should switch for GPU support then.

The GPU-enabled version of TensorFlow has several requirements such as 64-bit Linux, Python 2.7 (or 3.3+ for Python 3), NVIDIA CUDA® 7.5 or higher (CUDA 8.0 required for Pascal GPUs), and NVIDIA cuDNN v4.0 (minimum) or v5.1 (recommended). More specifically, the current development of TensorFlow supports only GPU computing using NVIDIA toolkits and software. Therefore, the following software must have to be installed on your Linux machine to get the GPU support on your predictive analytics applications:.

- Python
- NVIDIA Driver
- CUDA with **compute capability >= 3.0**
- CudNN
- TensorFlow

Installing Python and nVidia Driver

We have already seen how to install Python on a different platform, so we can skip this one. Also, I'm assuming that your machine already has a NVIDIA GPU installed.

To find out if your GPU is really installed properly and working, issue the following command on the terminal:

```
$ lspci -nnk | grep -i nvidia
# Expected output (of course may vary for your case): 4b:00.0 VGA
compatible controller [0300]: NVIDIA Corporation Device [10de:1b80] (rev
a1)4b:00.1 Audio device [0403]: NVIDIA Corporation Device [10de:10f0]
(rev a1)
```

Since predictive analytics largely depend on machine learning and deep learning algorithms, make sure you check that some essential packages are installed on your machine such as GCC and some of the scientific Python packages.

Simply issue the following command for doing so on the terminal:

```
$ sudo apt-get update
$ sudo apt-get install libglu1-mesa libxi-dev libxmu-dev -y
$ sudo apt-get — yes install build-essential
$ sudo apt-get install python-pip python-dev -y
$ sudo apt-get install python-numpy python-scipy -y
```

Now download the NVIDIA driver (don't forget to choose the right version for your machine) via `wget` and run the script in silent mode:

```
$ wget http://us.download.nvidia.com/XFree86/Linux-x86_64/367.44/NVIDIA-
Linux-x86_64-367.44.run
$ sudo chmod +x NVIDIA-Linux-x86_64-367.35.run
$ ./NVIDIA-Linux-x86_64-367.35.run --silent
```

 Some GPU cards such as NVidia GTX 1080 comes with the built in–driver. Thus, if your machine has a different GPU other than the GTX 1080, you have to download the driver for that GPU.

To make sure if the driver was installed correctly, issue the following command on the terminal:

```
$ nvidia-smi
```

The outcome of the command should be as follows:

```
ubuntu@ip-172-31-12-225:~$ nvidia-smi
Wed Sep 27 00:58:45 2017
+-----------------------------------------------------------------------------+
| NVIDIA-SMI 384.81                 Driver Version: 384.81                     |
|-------------------------------+----------------------+----------------------+
| GPU  Name        Persistence-M| Bus-Id        Disp.A | Volatile Uncorr. ECC |
| Fan  Temp  Perf  Pwr:Usage/Cap|         Memory-Usage | GPU-Util  Compute M. |
|===============================+======================+======================|
|   0  Tesla K80           Off  | 00000000:00:1E.0 Off |                    0 |
| N/A   48C    P0    59W / 149W |      0MiB / 11439MiB |     70%      Default |
+-------------------------------+----------------------+----------------------+

+-----------------------------------------------------------------------------+
| Processes:                                                       GPU Memory |
|  GPU       PID   Type   Process name                             Usage      |
|=============================================================================|
|  No running processes found                                                 |
+-----------------------------------------------------------------------------+
ubuntu@ip-172-31-12-225:~$
```

Figure 4: Outcome of the nvidia-smi command

Installing NVIDIA CUDA

To use TensorFlow with NVIDIA GPUs, CUDA® Toolkit 8.0, and associated NVIDIA drivers with CUDA toolkit 8+ are required to be installed. The CUDA toolkit includes:

- GPU-accelerated libraries such as cuFFT for **Fast Fourier Transforms (FFT)**
- cuBLAS for **Basic Linear Algebra Subroutines (BLAS)**
- cuSPARSE for sparse matrix routines

- cuSOLVER for dense and sparse direct solvers
- cuRAND for random number generation, NPP for image, and video processing primitives
- **nvGRAPH** for **NVIDIA Graph Analytics Library**
- Thrust for template parallel algorithms and data structures and a dedicated CUDA math library

For Linux, download and install required packages:

`https://developer.nvidia.com/cuda-downloads` using the `wget` command on Ubuntu as follows:

```
$ wget https://developer.nvidia.com/compute/cuda/8.0/Prod2/local_
installers/cuda_8.0.61_375.26_linux-run

$ sudo chmod +x cuda_8.0.61_375.26_linux.run

$ ./ cuda_8.0.61_375.26_linux.run --driver --silent

$ ./ cuda_8.0.61_375.26_linux.run --toolkit --silent

$ ./ cuda_8.0.61_375.26_linux.run --samples -silent
```

Also, ensure that you have added the CUDA installation path to the `LD_LIBRARY_PATH` environment variable as follows:

```
$ echo 'export LD_LIBRARY_PATH="$LD_LIBRARY_PATH:/usr/local/cuda/lib64:/
usr/local/cuda/extras/CUPTI/lib64"' >> ~/.bashrc

$ echo 'export CUDA_HOME=/usr/local/cuda' >> ~/.bashrc

$ source ~/.bashrc
```

Installing NVIDIA cuDNN v5.1+

Once the CUDA Toolkit is installed, you should download the cuDNN v5.1 library from `https://developer.nvidia.com/cudnn` for Linux and once downloaded, uncompress the files and copy them into the CUDA Toolkit directory (assumed here to be in /usr/local/cuda/):

```
$ cd /usr/local

$sudo mkdir cuda

$ cd ~/Downloads/

$ wget http://developer2.download.nvidia.com/compute/machine-learning/
cudnn/secure/v6/prod/8.0_20170427/cudnn-8.0-linux-x64-v6.0.tgz

$ sudo tar -xvzf cudnn-8.0-linux-x64-v6.0.tgz

$ cp cuda/lib64/* /usr/local/cuda/lib64/

$ cp cuda/include/cudnn.h /usr/local/cuda/include/
```

Note that to install the cuDNN v5.1 library, you must need to register for the Accelerated Computing Developer Program at `https://developer.nvidia.com/accelerated-computing-developer`. Now when you have installed the cuDNN v5.1 library, ensure that you create the `CUDA_HOME` environment variable.

Installing the libcupti-dev Library

Lastly, you need to have the libcupti-dev library installed on your machine. This is the NVIDIA CUDA that provides advanced profiling support. To install this library, issue the following command:

```
$ sudo apt-get install libcupti-dev
```

Installing TensorFlow

Refer to the following section for more step-by-step guidelines on how to install the latest version of TensorFlow for the CPU only and GPU supports with NVIDIA cuDNN and CUDA computing capability. You can install TensorFlow on your machine in a number of ways, such as using virtualenv, pip, Docker, and Anaconda. However, using Docker and Anaconda is a bit advanced and this is why we have decided to use pip and virtualenv instead.

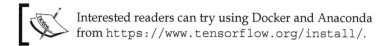 Interested readers can try using Docker and Anaconda from `https://www.tensorflow.org/install/`.

Installing TensorFlow with native pip

If steps 1 to 6 are completed, install TensorFlow by invoking one of the following commands. For Python 2.7 and, of course, with only CPU support:

```
$ pip install tensorflow
# For Python 3.x and of course with only CPU support:
$ pip3 install tensorflow
# For Python 2.7 and of course with GPU support:
$ pip install tensorflow-gpu
# For Python 3.x and of course with GPU support:

$ pip3 install tensorflow-gpu
```

If step 3 failed somehow, install the latest version of TensorFlow by issuing a command manually:

```
$ sudo pip install --upgrade TF_PYTHON_URL
#For Python 3.x, use the following command:
$ sudo pip3 install --upgrade TF_PYTHON_URL
```

For both cases, `TF_PYTHON_URL` signifies the URL of the TensorFlow Python package presented at https://www.tensorflow.org/install/install_linux#the_url_of_the_tensorflow_python_package.

For example, to install the latest version with CPU-only support (at the time of writing v1.1.0), use the following command:

```
$ sudo pip3 install --upgrade https://storage.googleapis.com/tensorflow/
linux/cpu/tensorflow-1.1.0-cp34-cp34m-linux_x86_64.wh
l
```

Installing with virtualenv

We assume that you already have Python 2+ (or 3+) and pip (or pip3) installed on your system. If so, follow these steps to install TensorFlow:

1. Create a virtualenv environment as follows:

   ```
   $ virtualenv --system-site-packages targetDirectory
   ```

   The `targetDirectory` signifies the root of the `virtualenv` tree. By default, it is `~/tensorflow` (however, you may choose any directory).

2. Activate virtualenv environment as follows:

   ```
   $ source ~/tensorflow/bin/activate # bash, sh, ksh, or zsh
     $ source ~/tensorflow/bin/activate.csh  # csh or tcsh
   ```

   If the command succeeds in step 2, then you should see the following on your terminal:

   ```
   (tensorflow)$
   ```

3. Installing TensorFlow.

   Follow one of the following commands to install TensorFlow in the active virtualenv environment. For Python 2.7 with CPU-only support, use the following command:

   ```
   (tensorflow)$ pip install --upgrade tensorflow
   #For Python 3.x with CPU support, use the following command:
   (tensorflow)$ pip3 install --upgrade tensorflow
   ```

```
#For Python 2.7 with GPU support, use the following command:
(tensorflow)$ pip install --upgrade tensorflow-gpu
#For Python 3.x with GPU support, use the following command:
 (tensorflow)$ pip3 install --upgrade tensorflow-gpu
```

If the preceding command succeeds, skip step 5. If the preceding command fails, perform step 5. Moreover, if step 3 failed somehow, try to install TensorFlow in the active virtualenv environment by issuing a command of the following format:

```
#For python 2.7 (select appropriate URL with CPU or GPU support):
(tensorflow)$ pip install --upgrade TF_PYTHON_URL
#For python 3.x (select appropriate URL with CPU or GPU support):
 (tensorflow)$ pip3 install --upgrade TF_PYTHON_URL
```

4. Validate the installation.

   To validate the installation in step 3, you must activate the virtual environment. If the virtualenv environment is not currently active, issue one of the following commands:

```
$ source ~/tensorflow/bin/activate   # bash, sh, ksh, or zsh
$ source ~/tensorflow/bin/activate.csh   # csh or tcsh
```

5. Uninstalling TensorFlow

   To uninstall TensorFlow, simply remove the tree you created. For example:

```
$ rm -r targetDirectory
```

   Finally, if you want to control which devices are visible to TensorFlow manually, you should set the CUDA_VISIBLE_DEVICES. For example, the following command can be used to force the use of only GPU 0:

```
$ CUDA_VISIBLE_DEVICES=0 python
```

Installing TensorFlow from Source

The pip installation can cause problems using TensorBoard (this will be discussed later in this lesson). For this reason, I suggest you build TensorFlow directly from the source. The steps are described as follows.

 Follow the instructions and guidelines on how to install Bazel on your platform at http://bazel.io/docs/install.html.

At first, clone the entire TensorFlow repository as follows:

```
$git clone --recurse-submodules https://github.com/tensorflow/tensorflow
```

Then it's time to install Bazel, which is a tool that automates software builds and tests. Also, for building TensorFlow from source, Bazel build system must be installed on your machine. For this, issue the following command:

```
$ sudo apt-get install software-properties-common swig
$ sudo add-apt-repository ppa:webupd8team/java
$ sudo apt-get update $ sudo apt-get install oracle-java8-installer
$ echo "deb http://storage.googleapis.com/bazel-apt stable jdk1.8" | sudo
tee /etc/apt/sources.list.d/bazel.list
$ curl https://storage.googleapis.com/bazel-apt/doc/apt-key.pub.gpg |
sudo apt-key add -
$ sudo apt-get update
$ sudo apt-get install bazel
```

Then run the Bazel installer by issuing the following command:

```
$ chmod +x bazel-version-installer-os.sh
$ ./bazel-version-installer-os.sh --user
```

Moreover, you might need some Python dependencies such as python-numpy, swig, and python-dev. Now, issue the following command for doing so:

```
$ sudo apt-get install python-numpy swig python-dev
```

Now it's time to configure the installation (GPU or CPU). Let's do it by executing the following command:

```
$ ./configure
```

Then create your TensorFlow package using bazel:

```
$ bazel build -c opt //tensorflow/tools/pip_package:
$ build_pip_package
```

However, to build with the GPU support, issue the following command:

```
$ bazel build -c opt --config=cuda //tensorflow/tools/pip_package:build_
pip_package
```

Finally, install TensorFlow. Here I have listed, as per the Python version:

- For Python 2.7:

```
$ sudo pip install --upgrade /tmp/tensorflow_pkg/
tensorflow-1.1.0-*.whl
```

- For Python 3.4:

```
$ sudo pip3 install --upgrade /tmp/tensorflow_pkg/
tensorflow-1.1.0-*.whl
```

Testing Your TensorFlow Installation

We start with the popular TensorFlow alias `tf`. Open a Python terminal (just type `python` or `python3` on terminal) and issue the following lines of code:

```
>>> import tensorflow as tf
```

If your favourite Python interpreter doesn't complain, then you're ready to start using TensorFlow!

```
>>> hello = tf.constant("Hello, TensorFlow!")
>>> sess=tf.Session()
```

Now to verify your installation just type the following:

```
>>> print sess.run(hello)
```

If the installation is OK, you'll see the following output:

```
Hello, TensorFlow!
```

TensorFlow Computational Graph

When thinking of execution of a TensorFlow program we should be familiar with a graph creation and a session execution. Basically the first one is for building the model and the second one is for feeding the data in and getting the results. An interesting thing is that TensorFlow does each and everything on the C++ engine, which means even a little multiplication or addition is not executed on Python but Python is just a wrapper. Fundamentally, TensorFlow C++ engine consists of following two things:

- Efficient implementations for operations like convolution, max pool, sigmoid, and so on.
- Derivatives of forwarding mode operation.

When we/you're performing a little complex operation with TensorFlow, for example training a linear regression, TensorFlow internally represents its computation using a dataflow graph. The graph is called a computational graph, which is a directed graph consisting of the following:

- A set of nodes, each one representing an operation
- A set of directed arcs, each one representing the data on which the operations are performed.

TensorFlow has two types of edges:

- **Normal**: They carry the data structures between the nodes. The output of one operation from one node, becomes input for another operation. The edge connecting two nodes carries the values.
- **Special**: This edge doesn't carry values, but only represents a control dependency between two nodes, say X and Y. It means that the node Y will be executed only if the operation in X is executed already, but before the relationship between operations on the data.

The TensorFlow implementation defines control dependencies to enforce orderings between otherwise independent operations as a way of controlling the peak memory usage.

A computational graph is basically like a dataflow graph. Figure 5 shows a computational graph for a simple computation like $z=d\times c=(a+b)\times c$:

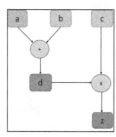

Figure 5: A very simple execution graph that computes a simple equation

In the preceding figure, the circles in the graph indicate the operations, while rectangles indicate a data computational graph. As stated earlier, a TensorFlow graph contains the following:

- **A set of tf.Operation objects**: This is used to represent units of computation to be performed
- **A tf.Tensor object**: This is used to represent units of data that control the dataflow between operations

Using TensorFlow, it is also possible to perform a deferred execution. To give an idea, once you have composed a highly compositional expression during the building phase of the computational graph, you can still evaluate them in the running session phase. Technically saying TensorFlow schedules the job and executes on time in an efficient manner. For example, parallel execution of independent parts of the code using the GPU is shown in figure 6.

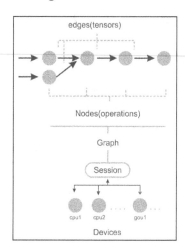

Figure 6: Edges and nodes in TensorFlow graph to be executed under a session on devices such as CPUs or GPUs

After a computational graph is created, TensorFlow needs to have an active session to be executed by multiple CPUs (and GPUs if available) in a distributed way. In general, you really don't need to specify whether to use a CPU or a GPU explicitly, since TensorFlow can choose and use which one is to be used. By default, a GPU will be picked for as many operations as possible; otherwise, a CPU will be used. So in a broad view, here are the main components of TensorFlow:

- **Variables**: Used to contain values for the weights and bias between TensorFlow sessions.

- **Tensors**: A set of values that pass in between nodes.

- **Placeholders**: Is used to send data between the program and the TensorFlow graph.

- **Session**: When a session is started, TensorFlow automatically calculates gradients for all the operations in the graph and use them in a chain rule. In fact, a session is invoked when the graph is to be executed.

Don't worry much, each of the preceding components will be discussed in later sections. Technically saying, the program you will be writing can be considered as a client. The client is then used to create the execution graph in C/C++ or Python symbolically, and then your code can ask TensorFlow to execute this graph. See details in the following figure:

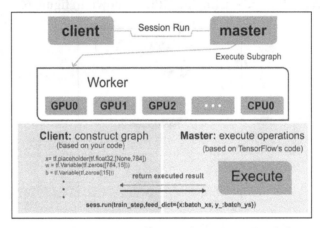

Figure 7: Using a client–master architecture for executing TensorFlow graph

A computational graph helps to distribute the work load across multiple computing nodes having a CPU or a GPU. This way, a neural network can further be equaled to a composite function where each layer (input, hidden or output layer) can be represented as a function. Now to understand the operations performed on the tensors, knowing a good workaround about TensorFlow programming model is a mandate. The next section explains the role of the computational graph to implement a neural network.

TensorFlow Programming Model

The TensorFlow programming model signifies how to structure your predictive models. A TensorFlow program is generally divided into four phases once you have imported TensorFlow library for associated resources:

- Construction of the computational graph that involves some operations on tensors (we will see what is a tensor soon)
- Create a session
- Running a session, that is performed for the operations defined in the graph
- Computation for data collection and analysis

These main steps define the programming model in TensorFlow. Consider the following example, in which we want to multiply two numbers:

```
import tensorflow as tf
x = tf.constant(8)
y = tf.constant(9)
z = tf.multiply(x, y)
sess = tf.Session()
out_z = sess.run(z)
Finally, close the TensorFlow session when you're done:

sess.close()print('The multiplicaiton of x and y: %d' % out_z)
```

The preceding code segment can be represented by the following figure:

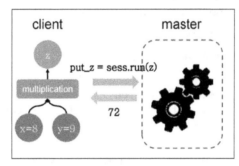

Figure 8: A simple multiplication executed and returned the product on client-master architecture

To make the preceding program more efficient, TensorFlow also allows you to exchange data in your graph variables through placeholders (to be discussed later). Now imagine the following code segment that does the same but in a more efficient way:

```
# Import tensorflow
import tensorflow as tf
# Build a graph and create session passing the graph:
with tf.Session() as sess:
 x = tf.placeholder(tf.float32, name="x")
 y = tf.placeholder(tf.float32, name="y")
 z = tf.multiply(x,y)
# Put the values 8,9 on the placeholders x,y and execute the graph
z_output = sess.run(z,feed_dict={x: 8, y:9})
# Finally, close the TensorFlow session when you're done:
sess.close()
print(z_output)
```

TensorFlow is not necessary to multiply two numbers; also the number of lines of the code for this simple operation is so many. However, the example wants to clarify how to structure any code, from the simplest as in this instance, to the most complex. Furthermore, the example also contains some basic instructions that we will find in all the other examples given in the course of this book.

> We will demonstrate most of the examples in this book with Python 3.x compatible. However, a few examples will be given using Python 2.7.x too.

This single import in the first line helps to import the TensorFlow for your command that can be instantiated with `tf as stated earlier. Then the TensorFlow` operator will then be expressed by `tf` and the dot `'.'` and by the name of the operator to use. In the next line, we construct the object `session`, by means of the instruction `tf.Session()`:

```
with tf.Session() as sess:
```

> The session object (that is, sess) encapsulates the environment for the TensorFlow so that all the operation objects are executed, and Tensor objects are evaluated. We will see them in upcoming sections.

This object contains the computation graph, which as we said earlier, are the calculations to be carried out.

The following two lines define variables x and y, using the notion of placeholder. Through a placeholder you may define both an input (such as the variable x of our example) and an output variable (such as the variable y):

```
x = tf.placeholder(tf.float32, name='x')
y = tf.placeholder(tf.float32, name='y')
```

Placeholder provides an interface between the elements of the graph and the computational data of the problem, it allows us to create our operations and build our computation graph, without needing the data, but only a reference to it.

To define a data or tensor (soon I will introduce you to the concept of tensor) via the placeholder function, three arguments are required:

- **Data type**: Is the type of element in the tensor to be fed.
- **Shape**: Of the placeholder–that is, shape of the tensor to be fed (optional). If the shape is not specified, you can feed a tensor of any shape.
- **Name**: Very useful for debugging and code analysis purposes, but it is optional.

For more, refer to `https://www.tensorflow.org/api_` `docs/python/tf/Tensor`.

So, we may introduce the model that we want to compute with two arguments, the placeholder and the constant that are previously defined. Next, we define the computational model.

The following statement, inside the session, builds the data structures of the x product with y, and the subsequent assignment of the result of the operation to the placeholder z. Then it goes as follows:

```
z = tf.multiply(x, y)
```

Now since the result is already held by the placeholder z, we execute the graph, through the `sess.run`statement. Here we feed two values to patch a tensor into a graph node. It temporarily replaces the output of an operation with a tensor value (more in upcoming sections):

```
z_output = sess.run(z,feed_dict={x: 8, y:9})
```

Then we close the TensorFlow session when we're done:

```
sess.close()
```

In the final instruction, we print out the result:

```
print(z_output)
```

This essentially prints output 72.0.

Data Model in TensorFlow

The data model in TensorFlow is represented by **tensors**. Without using complex mathematical definitions, we can say that a tensor (in TensorFlow) identifies a multidimensional numerical array. But we will see more details on tensor in the next sub-section.

Tensors

Let's see a formal definition of tensors from Wikipedia (`https://en.wikipedia.org/wiki/Tensor`) as follows:

"Tensors are geometric objects that describe linear relations between geometric vectors, scalars, and other tensors. Elementary examples of such relations include the dot product, the cross product, and linear maps. Geometric vectors, often used in physics and engineering applications, and scalars themselves are also tensors."

This data structure is characterized by three parameters: Rank, Shape, and Type, as shown in the following figure:

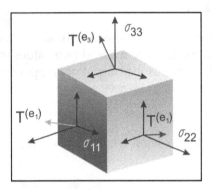

Figure 9: Tensors are nothing but geometrics objects having shape, rank, and type used to hold multidimensional arrays

A tensor thus can be thought of as a generalization of a matrix that specifies an element by an arbitrary number of indices. While practically used, the syntax for tensors is even more or less like nested vectors.

 Tensors just define the type of this value and the means by which this value should be calculated during the session. Therefore, essentially, they do not represent or hold any value produced by an operation.

A few people love to compare NumPy versus TensorFlow comparison; however, in reality, TensorFlow and NumPy are quite similar in a sense that both are N-d array libraries!

Well, it's true that NumPy has the n–dimensional array support, but it doesn't offer methods to create tensor functions and automatically compute derivatives (+ no GPU support). The following table can be seen as a short and one-to-one comparison that could make some sense of such comparisons:

Numpy	TensorFlow
a = np.zeros((2,2)); b = np.ones((2,2))	a = tf.zeros((2,2)), b = tf.ones((2,2))
np.sum(b, axis=1)	tf.reduce_sum(a,reduction_indices=[1])
a.shape	a.get_shape()
np.reshape(a, (1,4))	tf.reshape(a, (1,4))
b * 5 + 1	b * 5 + 1
np.dot(a,b)	tf.matmul(a, b)
a[0,0], a[:,0], a[0,:]	a[0,0], a[:,0], a[0,:]

Figure 10: NumPy versus TensorFlow

Now let's see an alternative way of creating tensors before they could be fed (we will see other feeding mechanisms later on) by the TensorFlow graph:

```
>>> X = [[2.0, 4.0],
         [6.0, 8.0]]
>>> Y = np.array([[2.0, 4.0],
                  [6.0, 6.0]], dtype=np.float32)
>>> Z = tf.constant([[2.0, 4.0],
                     [6.0, 8.0]])
```

Here X is a list, Y is an n-dimensional array from the NumPy library, and Z is itself the TensorFlow's Tensor object. Now let's see their types:

```
>>> print(type(X))
>>> print(type(Y))
>>> print(type(Z))
#Output
<class 'list'>
<class 'numpy.ndarray'>
<class 'tensorflow.python.framework.ops.Tensor'>
```

Well, their types are printed correctly. However, a more convenient function that we're formally dealing with tensors, as opposed to the other types is `tf.convert_to_tensor()` function as follows:

```
t1 = tf.convert_to_tensor(X, dtype=tf.float32)t2 = tf.convert_to_tensor(Z, dtype=tf.float32)t3 = tf.convert_to_tensor(Z, dtype=tf.float32)
```

Now let's see their type using the following lines:

```
>>> print(type(t1))
>>> print(type(t2))
>>> print(type(t3))
#Output:
<class 'tensorflow.python.framework.ops.Tensor'>
<class 'tensorflow.python.framework.ops.Tensor'>
<class 'tensorflow.python.framework.ops.Tensor'>
```

Fantastic! I think up to now it's enough discussion already carried out on tensors, so now we can think about the structure that is characterized by the term **rank**.

Rank

Each tensor is described by a unit of dimensionality called rank. It identifies the number of dimensions of the tensor, for this reason, a rank is known as order or n-dimensions of a tensor. A rank zero tensor is a scalar, a rank one tensor id a vector, while a rank two tensor is a matrix. The following code defines a TensorFlow scalar, a `vector`, a `matrix`, and a `cube_matrix`, in the next example we will show how the rank works:

```
import tensorflow as tf
scalar = tf.constant(100)
vector = tf.constant([1,2,3,4,5])
matrix = tf.constant([[1,2,3],[4,5,6]])
cube_matrix = tf.constant([[[1],[2],[3]],[[4],[5],[6]],[[7],[8],[9]]])
print(scalar.get_shape())
print(vector.get_shape())
print(matrix.get_shape())
print(cube_matrix.get_shape())
```

The results are printed here:

```
>>>
()
(5,)
(2, 3)
(3, 3, 1)
>>>
```

Shape

The shape of a tensor is the number of rows and columns it has. Now we will see how to relate the shape to a rank of a tensor:

```
>>scalar1.get_shape()
TensorShape([])
>>vector1.get_shape()
TensorShape([Dimension(5)])
>>matrix1.get_shape()
TensorShape([Dimension(2), Dimension(3)])
>>cube1.get_shape()
TensorShape([Dimension(3), Dimension(3), Dimension(1)])
```

Data Type

In addition to rank and shape, tensors have a data type. The following is the list of the data types:

Data type	Python type	Description
DT_FLOAT	tf.float32	32 bits floating point.
DT_DOUBLE	tf.float64	64 bits floating point.
DT_INT8	tf.int8	8 bits signed integer.
DT_INT16	tf.int16	16 bits signed integer.
DT_INT32	tf.int32	32 bits signed integer.
DT_INT64	tf.int64	64 bits signed integer.
DT_UINT8	tf.uint8	8 bits unsigned integer.
DT_STRING	tf.string	Variable length byte arrays. Each element of a tensor is a byte array.
DT_BOOL	tf.bool	Boolean.
DT_COMPLEX64	tf.complex64	Complex number made of two 32 bits floating points: real and imaginary parts.
DT_COMPLEX128	tf.complex128	Complex number made of two 64 bits floating points: real and imaginary parts.
DT_QINT8	tf.qint8	8 bits signed integer used in quantized Ops.
DT_QINT32	tf.qint32	32 bits signed integer used in quantized Ops.
DT_QUINT8	tf.quint8	8 bits unsigned integer used in quantized Ops.

We believe the preceding table is self-explanatory hence we did not provide detailed discussion on the preceding data types. Now the TensorFlow APIs are implemented to manage data **to** and **from** NumPy arrays. Thus, to build a tensor with a constant value, pass a NumPy array to the `tf.constant()` operator, and the result will be a TensorFlow tensor with that value:

```
import tensorflow as tf
import numpy as np
tensor_1d = np.array([1,2,3,4,5,6,7,8,9,10])
tensor_1d = tf.constant(tensor_1d)
```

```
with tf.Session() as sess:
    print (tensor_1d.get_shape())
    print sess.run(tensor_1d)
# Finally, close the TensorFlow session when you're done

sess.close()
```

Running the example, we obtain:

```
>>>
 (10,)
 [ 1  2  3  4  5  6  7  8  9 10]
```

To build a tensor, with variable values, use a `NumPy` array and pass it to the `tf.Variable` constructor, the result will be a TensorFlow variable tensor with that initial value:

```
import tensorflow as tf
import numpy as np
tensor_2d = np.array([(1,2,3),(4,5,6),(7,8,9)])
tensor_2d = tf.Variable(tensor_2d)
with tf.Session() as sess:
    sess.run(tf.global_variables_initializer())
    print (tensor_2d.get_shape())
    print sess.run(tensor_2d)
# Finally, close the TensorFlow session when you're done

sess.close()
```

The result is:

```
>>>
 (3, 3)
 [[1 2 3]
 [4 5 6]
 [7 8 9]]
```

For ease of use in interactive Python environments, we can use the `InteractiveSession` class, and then use that session for all `Tensor.eval()` and `Operation.run()` calls:

```
import tensorflow as tf
import numpy as np

interactive_session = tf.InteractiveSession()
tensor = np.array([1,2,3,4,5])
```

```
tensor = tf.constant(tensor)
print(tensor.eval())

interactive_session.close()
```

 tf.InteractiveSession() is just a convenient syntactic sugar for keeping a default session open in IPython.

The result is:

```
>>>
    [1 2 3 4 5]
```

This can be easier in an interactive setting, such as the shell or an IPython notebook, when it's tedious to pass around a session object everywhere.

 The IPython Notebook is now known as the Jupyter Notebook. It is an interactive computational environment, in which you can combine code execution, rich text, mathematics, plots and rich media. For more information, interested readers should refer to the web page at https://ipython.org/notebook.html.

Another way to define a tensor is using the TensorFlow statement tf.convert_to_tensor:

```
import tensorflow as tf
import numpy as np
tensor_3d = np.array([[[0, 1, 2], [3, 4, 5], [6, 7, 8]],
                      [[9, 10, 11], [12, 13, 14], [15, 16,
17]],
                      [[18, 19, 20], [21, 22, 23], [24, 25,
26]]])
tensor_3d = tf.convert_to_tensor(tensor_3d, dtype=tf.float64)
with tf.Session() as sess:
    print(tensor_3d.get_shape())
    print(sess.run(tensor_3d))
# Finally, close the TensorFlow session when you're done
sess.close()
>>>
(3, 3, 3)
[[[  0.   1.   2.]
  [  3.   4.   5.]
  [  6.   7.   8.]]
 [[  9.  10.  11.]
```

```
    [ 12.   13.   14.]
    [ 15.   16.   17.]]
 [[ 18.   19.   20.]
    [ 21.   22.   23.]
    [ 24.   25.   26.]]]
```

Variables

Variables are TensorFlow objects to hold and update parameters. A variable must be initialized; also you can save and restore it to analyze your code. Variables are created by using the `tf.Variable()` statement. In the following example, we want to count the numbers from 1 to 10, but let's import TensorFlow first:

```
import tensorflow as tf
```

We created a variable that will be initialized to the scalar value `0`:

```
value = tf.Variable(0, name="value")
```

The `assign()` and `add()` operators are just nodes of the computation graph, so they do not execute the assignment until the run of the session:

```
one = tf.constant(1)
new_value = tf.add(value, one)
update_value = tf.assign(value, new_value)
initialize_var = tf.global_variables_initializer()
```

We can instantiate the computation graph:

```
with tf.Session() as sess:
    sess.run(initialize_var)
    print(sess.run(value))
    for _ in range(5):
        sess.run(update_value)
        print(sess.run(value))
# Finally, close the TensorFlow session when you're done:

sess.close()
```

Let's recall that a tensor object is a symbolic handle to the result of an operation, but it does not actually hold the values of the operation's output:

```
>>>
0
1
2
3
4
5
```

Fetches

To fetch the outputs of operations, execute the graph by calling `run()` on the session object and pass in the tensors to retrieve. Except fetching the single tensor node, you can also fetch multiple tensors. In the following example, the sum and multiply tensors are fetched together, using the `run()` call:

```
import tensorflow as tf

constant_A = tf.constant([100.0])
constant_B = tf.constant([300.0])
constant_C = tf.constant([3.0])

sum_ = tf.add(constant_A,constant_B)
mul_ = tf.multiply(constant_A,constant_C)

with tf.Session() as sess:
    result = sess.run([sum_,mul_])
    print(result)

# Finally, close the TensorFlow session when you're done:

sess.close()
```

The output is as follows:

```
>>>

[array(400.],dtype=float32),array([ 300.],dtype=float32)]
```

All the ops needed to produce the values of the requested tensors are run once (not once per requested tensor).

Feeds and Placeholders

There are four methods of getting data into a TensorFlow program (see details at `https://www.tensorflow.org/api_guides/python/reading_data`):

- **The Dataset API**: This enables you to build complex input pipelines from simple and reusable pieces from distributed file systems and perform complex operations. Using the Dataset API is recommended while dealing with large amounts of data in different data formats. The Dataset API introduces two new abstractions to TensorFlow for creating feedable dataset using either `tf.contrib.data.Dataset` (by creating a source or applying a transformation operations) or using a `tf.contrib.data.Iterator`.

- **Feeding**: Allows us to inject data into any Tensor in a computation graph.

- **Reading from files**: We can develop an input pipeline using Python's built-in mechanism for reading data from data files at the beginning of a TensorFlow graph.

- **Preloaded data**: For small datasets, we can use either constants or variables in the TensorFlow graph for holding all the data.

In this section, we will see an example of the feeding mechanism only. For the other methods, we will see them in upcoming lesson. TensorFlow provides the feed mechanism that allows us inject data into any tensor in a computation graph. You can provide the feed data through the `feed_dict` argument to a `run()` or `eval()` invoke that initiates the computation.

> Feeding using the `feed_dict` argument is the least efficient way to feed data into a TensorFlow execution graph and should only be used for small experiments needing small datasets. It can also be used for debugging.

We can also replace any tensor with feed data (that is variables and constants), the best practice is to use a TensorFlow placeholder node using `tf.placeholder()` invocation. A placeholder exists exclusively to serve as the target of feeds. An empty placeholder is not initialized so it does not contain any data. Therefore, it will always generate an error if it is executed without a feed, so you won't forget to feed it.

The following example shows how to feed data to build a random 2×3 matrix:

```
import tensorflow as tf
import numpy as np

a = 3
b = 2
```

```
x = tf.placeholder(tf.float32,shape=(a,b))
y = tf.add(x,x)

data = np.random.rand(a,b)
sess = tf.Session()
print sess.run(y,feed_dict={x:data})

# Finally, close the TensorFlow session when you're done:

sess.close()
```

The output is:

```
>>>
[[ 1.78602004  1.64606333]
 [ 1.03966308  0.99269408]
 [ 0.98822606  1.50157797]]
>>>
```

TensorBoard

TensorFlow includes functions to debug and optimize programs in a visualization tool called **TensorBoard**. Using TensorBoard, you can observe different types of statistics concerning the parameters and details of any part of the graph computing graphically.

Moreover, while doing predictive modeling using the complex deep neural network, the graph can be complex and confusing. Thus to make it easier to understand, debug, and optimize TensorFlow programs, you can use TensorBoard to visualize your TensorFlow graph, plot quantitative metrics about the execution of your graph, and show additional data such as images that pass through it.

Therefore, the TensorBoard can be thought of as a framework designed for analysis and debugging of predictive models. TensorBoard uses the so-called summaries to view the parameters of the model: once a TensorFlow code is executed, we can call TensorBoard to view summaries in a GUI.

How Does TensorBoard Work?

As explained previously, TensorFlow uses the computation graph to execute an application, where each node represents an operation and the arcs are the data between operations.

The main idea in TensorBoard is to associate the so-called summary with nodes (operations) of the graph. Upon running the code, the summary operations will serialize the data of the node that is associated with it and output the data into a file that can be read by TensorBoard. Then TensorBoard can be run and visualize the summarized operations. The workflow when using TensorBoard is:

- Build your computational graph/code
- Attach summary ops to the nodes you are interested in examining
- Start running your graph as you normally would
- Additionally, run the summary ops
- When the code is done running, run TensorBoard to visualize the summary outputs

If you type `$ which tensorboard` in your terminal, it should exist if you installed with `pip`:

```
asif@ubuntu:~$ which tensorboard
/usr/local/bin/tensorboard
```

You need to give it a log directory, so you are in the directory where you ran your graph; you can launch it from your terminal with something like:

```
tensorboard --logdir .
```

Then open your favorite web browser and type in `localhost:6006` to connect. When TensorBoard is fully configured, this can be accessed by issuing the following command:

```
$ tensorboard -logdir=<trace_file_name>
```

Now you simply need to access the local port `6006` from the browser `http://localhost:6006/`. Then it should look like this:

Figure 11: Using TensorBoard on browser

Is this already too much? Don't worry, in the last section, we'll combine all the ideas previously explained to build a single input neuron model and to analyze it with TensorBoard.

Getting Started with TensorFlow – Linear Regression and Beyond

In this example, we will take a closer look at TensorFlow's and TensorBoard's main concepts and try to do some basic operations to get you started. The model we want to implement simulates the linear regression.

In the statistics and machine learning realm, linear regression is a technique frequently used to measure the relationship between variables. This is also a quite simple but effective algorithm that can be used in predictive modeling too. Linear regression models the relationship between a dependent variable **yi**, an interdependent variable **xi**, and a random term **b**. This can be seen as follows:

$$y = W * \mathrm{x} + \mathrm{b}$$

Now to conceptualize the preceding equation, I am going to write a simple Python program for creating data into a 2D space. Then I will use TensorFlow to look for the line that best fits in the data points:

```
# Import libraries (Numpy, matplotlib)
import numpy as np
import matplotlib.pyplot as plot

# Create 1000 points following a function y=0.1 * x + 0.4 (i.e. y \= W
* x + b) with some normal random distribution:

num_points = 1000
vectors_set = []
for i in range(num_points):
    W = 0.1 # W
    b = 0.4 # b
    x1 = np.random.normal(0.0, 1.0)
    nd = np.random.normal(0.0, 0.05)
    y1 = W * x1 + b

  # Add some impurity with some normal distribution -i.e. nd:
    y1 = y1+nd

  # Append them and create a combined vector set:
```

```
        vectors_set.append([x1, y1])

# Separate the data point across axises:
x_data = [v[0] for v in vectors_set]
y_data = [v[1] for v in vectors_set]

# Plot and show the data points in a 2D space
plt.plot(x_data, y_data, 'r*', label='Original data')
plt.legend()
plt.show()
```

If your compiler does not make any complaints, you should observe the following graph:

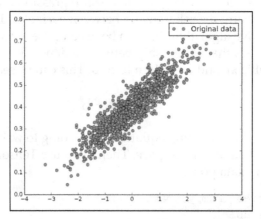

Figure 12: Randomly generated (but original) data

Well, so far we have just created a few data points without any associated model that could be executed through TensorFlow. So the next step is to create a linear regression model to be able to obtain the output values y that is estimated from the input data points–that is, x_data. In this context, we have only two associated parameters–that is, W and b. Now the objective is to create a graph that allows finding the values for these two parameters based on the input data x_data by adjusting them to y_data–that is, optimization problem.

So the target function in our case would be as follows:

$$y\_data = W * x\_data + b$$

If you recall, we defined **W = 0.1** and **b = 0.4** while creating the data points in the 2D space. Now TensorFlow has to optimize these two values so that w tends to 0.1 and b to 0.4, but without knowing any optimization function, TensorFlow does not even know anything.

A standard way to solve such optimization problems is to iterate through each value of the data points and adjust the value of `W` and `b` in order to get a more precise answer on each iteration. Now to realize if the values are really improving, we need to define a cost function that measures how good a certain line is.

In our case, the cost function is the mean squared error that helps find the average of the errors based on the distance function between the real data points and the estimated ones on each iteration. We start by importing the TensorFlow library:

```
import tensorflow as tf
W = tf.Variable(tf.random_uniform([1], -1.0, 1.0))
b = tf.Variable(tf.zeros([1]))
y = W * x_data + b
```

In the preceding code segment, we are generating a random point using a different strategy and storing in variable W. Now let's define a loss function **loss=mean [(y−y_data) 2]** and this returns a scalar value with the mean of all distances between our data and the model prediction. In terms of TensorFlow convention, the loss function can be expressed as follows:

```
loss = tf.reduce_mean(tf.square(y - y_data))
```

Without going into further detail, we can use some widely used optimization algorithms such as gradient descent. At a minimal level, the gradient descent is an algorithm that works on a set of given parameters that we already have. It starts with an initial set of parameter values and iteratively moves toward a set of values that minimize the function by taking another parameter called learning rate. This iterative minimization is achieved by taking steps in the negative direction of the function called gradient.

```
optimizer = tf.train.GradientDescentOptimizer(0.6)
train = optimizer.minimize(loss)
```

Before running this optimization function, we need to initialize all the variables that we have so far. Let's do it using TensorFlow convention as follows:

```
init = tf.global_variables_initializer()
sess = tf.Session()
sess.run(init)
```

Since we have created a TensorFlow session, we are ready for the iterative process that helps us find the optimal values of `W` and `b`:

```
for i in range(16):
    sess.run(train)
    print(i, sess.run(W), sess.run(b), sess.run(loss))
```

You should observe the following output:

```
>>>
0 [ 0.18418592]  [ 0.47198644]  0.0152888
1 [ 0.08373772]  [ 0.38146532]  0.00311204
2 [ 0.10470386]  [ 0.39876288]  0.00262051
3 [ 0.10031486]  [ 0.39547175]  0.00260051
4 [ 0.10123629]  [ 0.39609471]  0.00259969
5 [ 0.1010423]   [ 0.39597753]  0.00259966
6 [ 0.10108326]  [ 0.3959994]   0.00259966
7 [ 0.10107458]  [ 0.39599535]  0.00259966
```

Thus you can see the algorithm starts with the initial values of **W = 0.18418592 and b = 0.47198644** where the loss is pretty high. Then the algorithm iteratively adjusted the values by minimizing the cost function. In the eighth iteration, all the values tend to our desired values.

Now what if we could plot them? Let's do it by adding the plotting line under the `for` loop as follows:

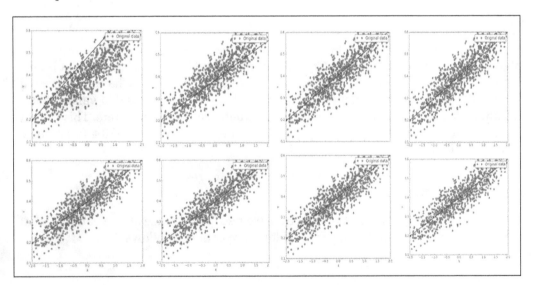

Figure 13: Linear regression after eight iteration that optimizes the loss function

Now let's iterate the same up to the 16th iteration:

```
>>>
0 [ 0.23306453]  [ 0.47967502]  0.0259004
1 [ 0.08183448]  [ 0.38200468]  0.00311023
2 [ 0.10253634]  [ 0.40177572]  0.00254209
3 [ 0.09969243]  [ 0.39778906]  0.0025257
```

```
 4 [ 0.10008509] [ 0.39859086] 0.00252516
 5 [ 0.10003048] [ 0.39842987] 0.00252514
 6 [ 0.10003816] [ 0.39846218] 0.00252514
 7 [ 0.10003706] [ 0.39845571] 0.00252514
 8 [ 0.10003722] [ 0.39845699] 0.00252514
 9 [ 0.10003719] [ 0.39845672] 0.00252514
10 [ 0.1000372] [ 0.39845678] 0.00252514
11 [ 0.1000372] [ 0.39845678] 0.00252514
12 [ 0.1000372] [ 0.39845678] 0.00252514
13 [ 0.1000372] [ 0.39845678] 0.00252514
14 [ 0.1000372] [ 0.39845678] 0.00252514
15 [ 0.1000372] [ 0.39845678] 0.00252514
```

Much better and we're closer to the optimized values, right? Now, what if we further improve our visual analytics through TensorFlow that help visualize what is happening in these graphs. TensorBoard provides a web page for debugging your graph as well as inspecting the used variables, node, edges, and their corresponding connections.

However, to get the facility of the preceding regression analysis, you need to annotate the preceding graphs with the variables such as loss function, `W`, `b`, `y_data`, `x_data`, and so on. Then you need to generate all the summaries by invoking the function `tf.summary.merge_all()`.

Now, we need to make the following changes to the preceding code. However, it is a good practice to group related nodes on the graph using the `tf.name_scope()` function. Thus, we can use `tf.name_scope()` to organize things on the TensorBoard graph view, but let's give it a better name:

```
with tf.name_scope("LinearRegression") as scope:
    W = tf.Variable(tf.random_uniform([1], -1.0, 1.0), name="Weights")
    b = tf.Variable(tf.zeros([1]))y = W * x_data + b
```

Then let's annotate the loss function in a similar way, but by giving a suitable name such as `LossFunction`:

```
with tf.name_scope("LossFunction") as scope:
    loss = tf.reduce_mean(tf.square(y - y_data))
```

Let's annotate the loss, weights, and bias that are needed for the TensorBoard:

```
loss_summary = tf.summary.scalar("loss", loss)
w_ = tf.summary.histogram("W", W)
b_ = tf.summary.histogram("b", b)
```

Well, once you annotate the graph, it's time to configure the summary by merging them:

```
merged_op = tf.summary.merge_all()
```

Now before running the training (after the initialization), write the summary using the `tf.summary.FileWriter()` API as follows:

```
writer_tensorboard = tf.summary.FileWriter('/home/asif/LR/', sess.
graph_def)
```

Then start the TensorBoard as follows:

$ tensorboard -logdir=<trace_file_name>

In our case, it could be something like the following:

$ tensorboard --logdir=/home/asif/LR/

Now let's move to `http://localhost:6006` and on clicking on the **GRAPHS** tab, you should see the following graph:

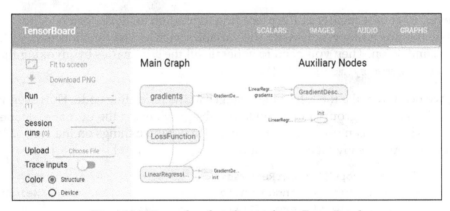

Figure 14: Main graph and auxiliary nodes on TensorBoard

Source Code for the Linear Regression

We reported for the entire source code for the example previously described:

```
# Import libraries (Numpy, Tensorflow, matplotlib)
import numpy as np
import matplotlib.pyplot as plot

# Create 1000 points following a function y=0.1 * x + 0.4 (i.e. y = W
* x + b) with some normal random distribution:
num_points = 1000
vectors_set = []
```

```
for i in range(num_points):
    W = 0.1  # W
    b = 0.4  # b
    x1 = np.random.normal(0.0, 1.0)
    nd = np.random.normal(0.0, 0.05)
    y1 = W * x1 + b

# Add some impurity with some normal distribution -i.e. nd:y1 = y1 +
nd
```

```
# Append them and create a combined vector set:
    vectors_set.append([x1, y1])

# Separate the data point across axises
x_data = [v[0] for v in vectors_set]
y_data = [v[1] for v in vectors_set]

# Plot and show the data points in a 2D space
plot.plot(x_data, y_data, 'ro', label='Original data')
plot.legend()
plot.show()

import tensorflow as tf

#tf.name_scope organize things on the tensorboard graph view
with tf.name_scope("LinearRegression") as scope:
    W = tf.Variable(tf.random_uniform([1], -1.0, 1.0), name="Weights")
    b = tf.Variable(tf.zeros([1]))
    y = W * x_data + b

# Define a loss function that takes into account the distance between
the prediction and our dataset
with tf.name_scope("LossFunction") as scope:
    loss = tf.reduce_mean(tf.square(y - y_data))

optimizer = tf.train.GradientDescentOptimizer(0.6)
train = optimizer.minimize(loss)

# Annotate loss, weights, and bias (Needed for tensorboard)
loss_summary = tf.summary.scalar("loss", loss)
w_ = tf.summary.histogram("W", W)
b_ = tf.summary.histogram("b", b)

# Merge all the summaries
```

```
merged_op = tf.summary.merge_all()

init = tf.global_variables_initializer()
sess = tf.Session()
sess.run(init)

# Writer for TensorBoard  (replace with our preferred location
writer_tensorboard = tf.summary.FileWriter('/ LR/', sess.graph_def)

for i in range(16):
    sess.run(train)
    print(i, sess.run(W), sess.run(b), sess.run(loss))
    plot.plot(x_data, y_data, 'ro', label='Original data')
    plot.plot(x_data, sess.run(W)*x_data + sess.run(b))
    plot.xlabel('X')
    plot.xlim(-2, 2)
    plot.ylim(0.1, 0.6)
    plot.ylabel('Y')
    plot.legend()
    plot.show()
# Finally, close the TensorFlow session when you're done

sess.close()
```

Ubuntu may ask you to install the python-tk package. You can do it by executing the following command on Ubuntu:

```
$ sudo apt-get install python-tk
# For Python 3.x, use the following
$ sudo apt-get install python3-tk
```

Summary

TensorFlow is designed to make the predictive analytics through the machine and deep learning easy for everyone, but using it does require understanding some general principles and algorithms. Furthermore, the latest release of TensorFlow comes with lots of exciting features. Thus I also tried to cover them so that you can use them with ease. I have shown how to install TensorFlow on different platforms including Linux, Windows, and Mac OS. In summary, here is a brief recap of the key concepts of TensorFlow explained in this lesson:

- **Graph**: each TensorFlow computation can be represented as a set of dataflow graphs where each graph is built as a set of operation objects. There are three core graph data structures:
    1. `tf.Graph`
    2. `tf.Operation`
    3. `tf.Tensor`

- **Operation**: A graph node takes tensors as input and also produces a tensor as output. A node can be represented by an operation object for performing units of computations such as addition, multiplication, division, subtraction or more complex operation.

- **Tensor**: Tensors are like high-dimensional array objects. In other words, they can be represented as edges of a dataflow graph but still they don't hold any value produced out of an operations.

- **Session**: A session object is an entity that encapsulates the environment in which operation objects are executed for running calculations on the dataflow graph. As a result, the tensors objects are evaluated inside the `run()` or `eval()` invocation.

In a later section of the lesson, we introduced TensorBoard, which is a powerful tool for analyzing and debugging neural network models, the lesson ended with an example that shows how to implement a simple neuron model and how to analyze its learning phase with TensorBoard.

Predictive models often perform calculations during live transactions, for example, to evaluate the risk or opportunity of a given customer or transaction, in order to guide a decision. With advancements in computing speed, individual agent modeling systems have become capable of simulating human behavior or reactions to given stimuli or scenarios.

In the next lesson, we will cover linear models for regression, classification, and clustering and dimensionality reduction and will also give some insights about some performance measures.

Assessments

1. Each tensor is described by a unit of dimensionality called ____.

    1. Data type

    2. Rank

    3. Variables

    4. Fetches

2. State whether the following statement is True or False: TensorFlow uses the computation graph to execute an application, where each node represents an operation and the arcs are the data between operations.

3. State whether the following statement is True or False: NumPy has the n–dimensional array support, but it doesn't offer methods to create tensor functions and automatically compute derivatives (+ no GPU support).

4. Which objects does a TensorFlow graph contains?

5. When you're performing a little complex operation with TensorFlow, for example training a linear regression, TensorFlow internally represents its computation using a dataflow graph. The graph is called as?

    1. Dataflow graph

    2. Linear graph

    3. Computational graph

    4. Regression graph

2

Putting Data in Place – Supervised Learning for Predictive Analytics

In this lesson, we will discuss supervised learning from the theoretical and practical perspective. In particular, we will revisit the linear regression model for regression analysis discussed in *Lesson 1*, *From Data to Decisions – Getting Started with TensorFlow*, using a real dataset. Then we will see how to develop Titanic survival predictive models using **Logistic Regression (LR)**, Random Forests, and **Support Vector Machines (SVMs)**.

In a nutshell, the following topics will be covered in this lesson:

- Supervised learning for predictive analytics
- Linear regression for predictive analytics: revisited
- Logistic regression for predictive analytics
- Random forests for predictive analytics
- SVMs for predictive analytics
- A comparative analysis

Supervised Learning for Predictive Analytics

Depending on the nature of the learning feedback available, the machine learning process is typically classified into three broad categories: supervised learning, unsupervised learning, and reinforcement learning—see figure 1. A predictive model based on supervised learning algorithms can make predictions based on a labelled dataset that map inputs to outputs aligning with the real world.

For example, a dataset for spam filtering usually contains spam messages as well as not-spam messages. Therefore, we could know which messages in the training set are spam and which are ham. Nevertheless, we might have the opportunity to use this information to train our model in order to classify new unseen messages:

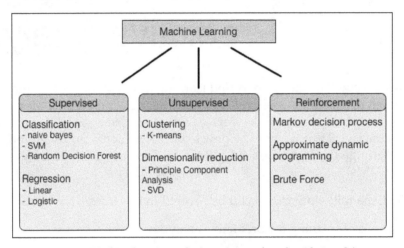

Figure 1: Machine learning tasks (containing a few algorithms only)

The following figure shows the schematic diagram of supervised learning. After the algorithm has found the required patterns, those patterns can be used to make predictions for unlabeled test data:

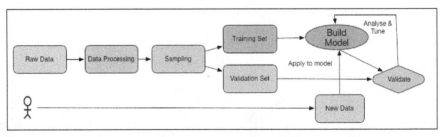

Figure 2: Supervised learning in action

Examples include classification and regression for solving supervised learning problems so that predictive models can be built for predictive analytics based on them. We will provide several examples of supervised learning like linear regression, logistic regression, random forest, decision trees, Naive Bayes, multilayer perceptron, and so on.

In this lesson, we will mainly focus on the supervised learning algorithms for predictive analytics. Let's start from the very simple linear regression algorithm.

Linear Regression – Revisited

In *Lesson 1, From Data to Decisions – Getting Started with TensorFlow* we have seen an example of linear regression. We have observed how to work TensorFlow on the randomly generated dataset, that is, fake data. We have seen that the regression is a type of supervised machine learning for predicting the continuous-valued output. However, running a linear regression on fake data is just like buying a new car and never driving it. This awesome machinery begs to manifest itself in the real world!

Fortunately, many datasets are available online to test your new-found knowledge of regression:

- The University of Massachusetts Amherst supplies small datasets of various types: http://www.umass.edu/statdata/statdata/

- Kaggle contains all types of large-scale data for machine learning competitions: https://www.kaggle.com/datasets

- Data.gov is an open data initiative by the US government, which contains many interesting and practical datasets: https://catalog.data.gov

Therefore, in this section, by defining a set of models, we will see how to reduce the search space of possible functions. Moreover, TensorFlow takes advantage of the differentiable property of the functions by running its efficient gradient descent optimizers to learn the parameters. To avoid overfitting our data, we regularize the cost function by penalizing larger valued parameters.

The linear regression is shown in *Lesson 1, From Data to Decision – Getting Started with TensorFlow*, shows some tensors that just contained a single scalar value, but you can, of course, perform computations on arrays of any shape. In TensorFlow, operations such as addition and multiplication take two inputs and produce an output. In contrast, constants and variables do not take any input. We will also see an example of how TensorFlow can manipulate 2D arrays to perform linear regression like operations.

Problem Statement

Online movie ratings and recommendations have become a serious business around the world. For example, Hollywood generates about $10 billion at the U.S. box office each year. Websites like Rotten Tomatoes aggregates movie reviews into one overall rating and also reports poor opening weekends. Although a single movie critic or a single negative review can't make or break a film, thousands of reviews and critics do.

Rotten Tomatoes, Metacritic, and IMDb have their own way of aggregating film reviews and distinct rating systems. On the other hand, Fandango, an NBCUniversal subsidiary uses a five-star rating system in which most of the movies get at least three stars, according to a FiveThirtyEight analysis.

An exploratory analysis of the dataset used by Fandango shows that out of 510 films, 437 films got at least one review where, hilariously, 98% had a 3-star rating or higher and 75 percent had a 4-star rating or higher. This implies, that using Fandango's standards it's almost impossible for a movie to be a flop at the box office. Therefore, Fandango's rating is biased and skewed:

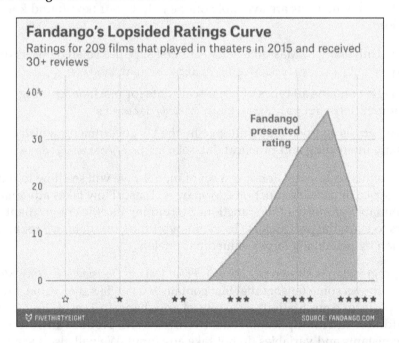

Figure 3: Fandango's lopsided ratings curve

(Source: https://fivethirtyeight.com/features/fandango-movies-ratings/)

Since the ratings from Fandango are unreliable, we will instead predict our own ratings based on IMDb ratings. More specifically, this is a multivariate regression problem, since our predictive model will use multiple features to make the rating prediction having many predictors.

Fortunately, the data is small enough to fit in memory, so plain batch learning should do just fine. Considering these factors and need, we will see that linear regression will meet our requirements. However, for more robust regression, you can still use deep neural network based regression techniques such as deep belief networks Regressor.

Using Linear Regression for Movie Rating Prediction

Now, the first task is downloading the Fandango's rating dataset from GitHub at `https://github.com/fivethirtyeight/data/tree/master/fandango`. It contains every film that has a Rotten Tomatoes rating, an RT user rating, a Metacritic score, a Metacritic user score, IMDb score, and at least 30 fan reviews on Fandango.

The dataset has 22 columns that can be described as follows:

Column	Definition
FILM	Name of the film.
RottenTomatoes	Corresponding Tomatometer score for the film by Rotten Tomatoes.
RottenTomatoes_User	Rotten Tomatoes user score for the film.
Metacritic	Metacritic critic score for the film.
Metacritic_User	Metacritic user score for the film.
IMDB	IMDb user score for the film.
Fandango_Stars	A number of stars the film had on its Fandango movie page.
Fandango_Ratingvalue	The Fandango rating value for the film, as pulled from the HTML of each page. This is the actual average score the movie obtained.
RT_norm	Tomatometer score for the film. It is normalized to a 0 to 5 point system.
RT_user_norm	Rotten Tomatoes user score for the film. It is normalized to a 0 to 5 point system.

Metacritic_norm	The Metacritic critic scores for the film. It is normalized to a 0 to 5 point system.
Metacritic_user_nom	Metacritic user score for the film, normalized to a 0 to 5 point system.
IMDB_norm	IMDb user score for the film which is normalized to a 0 to 5 point system.
RT_norm_round	Rotten Tomatoes Tomatometer score for the film which is normalized to a 0 to 5 point system and rounded to the nearest half-star.
RT_user_norm_round	Rotten Tomatoes user score for the film, normalized to a 0 to 5 point system and rounded to the nearest half-star.
Metacritic_norm_round	Metacritic critic score for the film, normalized to a 0 to 5 point system and rounded to the nearest half-star.
Metacritic_user_norm_round	Metacritic user score for the film, normalized to a 0 to 5 point system and rounded to the nearest half-star.
IMDB_norm_round	IMDb user score for the film, normalized to a 0 to 5 point system and rounded to the nearest half-star.
Metacritic_user_vote_count	A number of user votes the film had on Metacritic.
IMDB_user_vote_count	A number of user votes the film had on IMDb.
Fandango_votes	A number of user votes the film had on Fandango.
Fandango_Difference	Difference between the presented Fandango_Stars and the actual Fandango_Ratingvalue.

Table 1: Description of the columns in fandango_score_comparison.csv

We have already seen that a typical linear regression problem using TensorFlow has the following workflow that updates the parameters to minimize the given cost function of Fandango's lopsided rating curve:

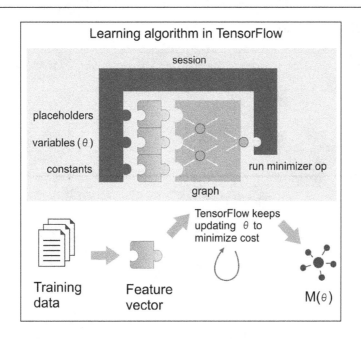

Figure 4: The learning algorithm using linear regression in TensorFlow

Now, let's try to follow the preceding figure and reproduce the same for the linear regression:

1. Import the required libraries:

```
import numpy as np
import pandas as pd
from scipy import stats
import sklearn
from sklearn.model_selection import train_test_split
import tensorflow as tf
import matplotlib
import matplotlib.pyplot as plt
import seaborn as sns
```

2. Read the dataset and create a Panda DataFrame:

```
df = pd.read_csv('fandango_score_comparison.csv')
print(df.head())
```

The output is as follows:

Fandango_Ratingvalue	RT_norm	RT_user_norm	Metacritic_norm	Metacritic_user_nom	IMDB_norm	RT_norm_round
4.5	3.7	4.3	3.3	3.55	3.9	3.5
4.5	4.25	4	3.35	3.75	3.55	4.5
4.5	4	4.5	3.2	4.05	3.9	4
4.5	0.9	4.2	1.1	2.35	2.7	1
3	0.7	1.4	1.45	1.7	2.55	0.5
4	3.15	3.1	2.5	3.4	3.6	3
3.5	2.1	2.65	2.65	3.8	3.45	2
3.5	4.3	3.2	4.05	3.4	3.25	4.5
4	4.95	4.1	4.05	4.4	3.7	5
4	4.45	4.35	4	4.25	3.9	4.5

Figure 5: A snap of the dataset showing a typo in the Metacritic_user_nom

So, if you look at the preceding DataFrame carefully, there is a typo that could cause a disaster. From our intuition, it is clear that `Metacritic_user_nom` should have actually been `Metacritic_user_norm`. Let's rename it to avoid further confusion:

```
df.rename(columns={'Metacritic_user_nom':'Metacritic_user_norm'},
inplace=True)
```

Moreover, according to a statistical analysis at `https://fivethirtyeight.com/features/fandango-movies-ratings/`, all the variables don't contribute equally; the following columns have more importance in ranking the movies:

```
 'Fandango_Stars',
'RT_user_norm',
'RT_norm',
'IMDB_norm',
'Metacritic_user_norm',
'Metacritic_norm'
```

Now we can check the correlation coefficients between variables before build the LR model. First, let's create a ranking list for that:

```
rankings_lst = ['Fandango_Stars',
                'RT_user_norm',
                'RT_norm',
                'IMDB_norm',
                'Metacritic_user_norm',
                'Metacritic_norm']
```

The following function computes the `Pearson` correlation coefficients and builds a full correlation matrix:

```
def my_heatmap(df):
    import seaborn as sns
    fig, axes = plt.subplots()
    sns.heatmap(df, annot=True)
    plt.show()
    plt.close()
```

Let's call the preceding method to plot the matrix as follows:

```
my_heatmap(df[rankings_lst].corr(method='pearson'))
```

 Pearson correlation coefficients: A measure of the strength of the linear relationship between two variables. If the relationship between the variables is not linear, then the correlation coefficient cannot accurately and adequately represent the strength of the relationship between those two variables. It is often represented as "ρ" when measured on population and "r" when measured on a sample. Statistically, the range is -1 to 1, where -1 indicates a perfect negative linear relationship, an r of 0 indicates no linear relationship, and an r of 1 indicates a perfect positive linear relationship between variables.

The following correlation matrix shows correlation between considered features using the Pearson correlation coefficients:

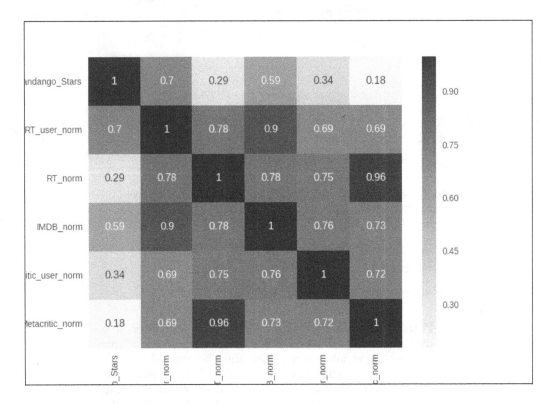

Figure 6: The correlation matrix on the ranking list movies

So, the correlation between Fandango and Metacritic is still positive. Now, let's do another study by considering only the movies for which RT has provided at least a 4-star rating:

```
RT_lst = df['RT_norm'] >= 4.
my_heatmap(df[RT_lst][rankings_lst].corr(method='pearson'))
>>>
```

The output is the correlation matrix on the ranked movies and RT movies having ratings of at least 4 showing a correlation between considered features using the Pearson correlation coefficients:

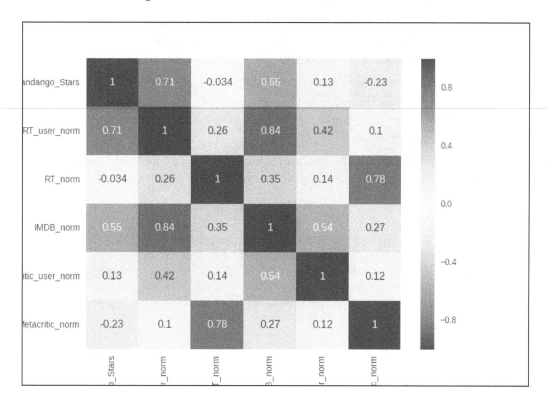

Figure 7: The correlation matrix on the ranked movies and RT movies having ratings at least 4

This time, we have obtained anticorrelation (that is, negative correlation) between Fandango and Metacritic, with the correlation coefficient-0.23. This means that the correlation of Metacritic in terms of Fandango is significantly biased toward high ratings.

Therefore, we can train our model without considering Fandango's rating, but before that let's build the LR model using this first. Later on, we will decide which option would produce a better result eventually.

3. Preparing the training and test sets.

Let's create a feature matrix X by selecting two DataFrame columns:

```
feature_cols = ['Fandango_Stars', 'RT_user_norm', 'RT_norm',
'Metacritic_user_norm', 'Metacritic_norm']
X = df.loc[:, feature_cols]
```

Here, I have used only the selected column as features and now we need to create a response vector y:

```
y = df['IMDB_norm']
```

We are assuming that the IMDB is the most reliable and the baseline source of ratings. Our ultimate target is to predict the rating of each movie and compare the predicted ratings with the response column IMDB_norm.

Now that we have the features and the response columns, it's time to split data into training and testing sets:

```
X_train, X_test, y_train, y_test = train_test_split(X, y, test_
size=0.50, random_state=43)
```

If you want to change the random_state, it helps you generate pseudo-random numbers for a random sampling value to obtain different final results.

 Random state: As the name sounds can be used for initializing the internal random number generator, which will decide the splitting of data into train and test indices. This also signifies that every time you run it without specifying random_state, you will get a different result, this is expected behavior. So, we can have the following three options:

- If random_state is None (or np.random), a randomly-initialized RandomState object is returned

- If random_state is an integer, it is used to seed a new RandomState object

- If random_state is a RandomState object, it is passed through

Now, we need to have the dimension of the dataset to be passed through the tensors:

```
dim = len(feature_cols)
```

We need to include an extra dimension for independent coefficient:

```
dim += 1
```

And so we need to create an extra column for the independent coefficient in the training set and test feature set as well:

```
X_train = X_train.assign( independent = pd.Series([1] * len(y_
train), index=X_train.index))
X_test = X_test.assign( independent = pd.Series([1] * len(y_
train), index=X_test.index))
```

So far, we have used and utilized the panda DataFrames but converting it into tensors is troublesome so instead let's convert them into a NumPy array:

```
P_train = X_train.as_matrix(columns=None)
P_test = X_test.as_matrix(columns=None)

q_train = np.array(y_train.values).reshape(-1,1)
q_test = np.array(y_test.values).reshape(-1,1)
```

4. Creating a place holder for TensorFlow.

   Now that we have all the training and test sets, before initializing these variables, we have to create the place holder for TensorFlow to feed the training sets across the tensors:

   ```
   P = tf.placeholder(tf.float32, [None,dim])
   q = tf.placeholder(tf.float32, [None,1])
   T = tf.Variable(tf.ones([dim,1]))
   ```

   Let's add some bias to differing from the value in the case where both types are quantized as follows:

   ```
   bias = tf.Variable(tf.constant(1.0, shape = [n_dim]))
   q_ = tf.add(tf.matmul(P, T),bias)
   ```

5. Creating an optimizer.

   Let's create an optimizer for the objective function:

   ```
   cost = tf.reduce_mean(tf.square(q_ - q))
   learning_rate = 0.0001
   training_op = tf.train.GradientDescentOptimizer(learning_
   rate=learning_rate).minimize(cost)
   ```

6. Initializing global variables:

   ```
   init_op = tf.global_variables_initializer()
   cost_history = np.empty(shape=[1],dtype=float)
   ```

7. Training the LR model.

   Here we are iterating the training 50,000 times and tracking several parameters, such as means square error that signifies how good the training is; we are keeping the cost history for future visualization, and so on:

   ```
   training_epochs = 50000
   with tf.Session() as sess:
       sess.run(init_op)
       cost_history = np.empty(shape=[1], dtype=float)
       t_history = np.empty(shape=[dim, 1], dtype=float)
       for epoch in range(training_epochs):
           sess.run(training_op, feed_dict={P: P_train, q: q_train})
   ```

```
        cost_history = np.append(cost_history, sess.run(cost,
feed_dict={P: P_train, q: q_train}))
        t_history = np.append(t_history, sess.run(T, feed_dict={P:
P_train, q: q_train}), axis=1)
    q_pred = sess.run(q_, feed_dict={P: P_test})[:, 0]
    mse = tf.reduce_mean(tf.square(q_pred - q_test))
    mse_temp = mse.eval()
    sess.close()
```

Finally, we evaluate the `mse` to get the scalar value out of the training evaluation on the test set. Now, let's compute the `mse` and `rmse` values, as follows:

```
print(mse_temp)
RMSE = math.sqrt(mse_temp)
print(RMSE)
>>>
0.425983107542
0.6526738140461913
```

You can also change the feature column, as follows:

```
feature_cols = ['RT_user_norm', 'RT_norm', 'Metacritic_user_norm',
'Metacritic_norm']
```

Now that we are not considering the Fandango's stars, I experienced the following result of `mse` and `rmse` respectively:

```
0.426362842426
0.6529646563375979
```

8. Observing the training cost throughout iterations:

```
fig, axes = plt.subplots()
plt.plot(range(len(cost_history)), cost_history)
axes.set_xlim(xmin=0.95)
axes.set_ylim(ymin=1.e-2)
axes.set_xscale("log", nonposx='clip')
axes.set_yscale("log", nonposy='clip')
axes.set_ylabel('Training cost')
axes.set_xlabel('Iterations')
axes.set_title('Learning rate = ' + str(learning_rate))
plt.show()
plt.close()
>>>
```

The output is as follows:

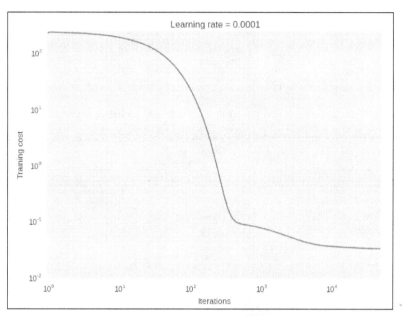

Figure 8: The training and training cost become saturated after 10000 iterations

The preceding graph shows that the training cost becomes saturated after 10,000 iterations. This also means that, even if you iterate the model more than 10,000 times, the cost is not going to experience a significant decrease.

9. Evaluating the model:

```
predictedDF = X_test.copy(deep=True)
predictedDF.insert(loc=0, column='IMDB_norm_predicted', value=pd.
Series(data=q_pred, index=predictedDF.index))
predictedDF.insert(loc=0, column='IMDB_norm_actual', value=q_test)

print('Predicted vs actual rating using LR with TensorFlow')
print(predictedDF[['IMDB_norm_actual', 'IMDB_norm_predicted']].
head())print(predictedDF[['IMDB_norm_actual', 'IMDB_norm_
predicted']].tail())
>>>
```

The following shows the predicted versus actual rating using LR:

	IMDB_norm_actual	IMDB_norm_predicted
45	3.30	3.232061
50	3.35	3.381659
98	3.05	2.869175

119	3.60	3.796200
133	2.15	2.521702
140	4.30	4.033006
143	3.70	3.816177
42	4.10	3.996275
90	3.05	3.226954
40	3.45	3.509809

We can see that the prediction is a continuous value. Now it's time to see how well the LR model generalizes and fits to the regression line:

```
How the LR fit with the predicted data points:
plt.scatter(q_test, q_pred, color='blue', alpha=0.5)
plt.plot([q_test.min(), q_test.max()], [q_test.min(), q_test.
max()], '--', lw=1)
plt.title('Predicted vs Actual')
plt.xlabel('Actual')
plt.ylabel('Predicted')
plt.show()
plt.show()


>>>
```

The output is as follows:

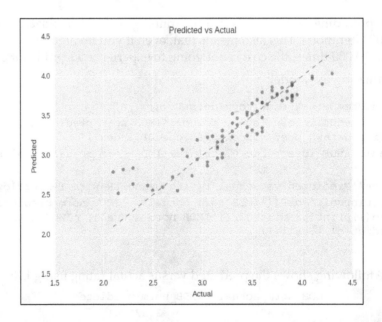

Figure 9: Prediction made by the LR model

The graph does not tell us that the prediction made by the LR model is good or bad. But we can still improve the performance of such models using layer architectures such as deep neural networks.

The next example is about applying other supervised learning algorithms such as logistic regression, support vector machines, and random forest for predictive analytics.

From Disaster to Decision – Titanic Example Revisited

In *Lesson 1, From Data to Decisions – Getting Started with TensorFlow*, we have seen a minimal data analysis of the Titanic dataset. Now it's our turn to do some analytics on top of the data. Let's look at what kinds of people survived the disaster.

Since we have enough data, but how could we do the predictive modeling so that we can draw some fairly straightforward conclusions from this data? For example, being a woman, being in first class, and being a child were all factors that could boost a passengers chances of survival during this disaster.

Using the brute-force approach such as if-else statements with some sort of weighted scoring system, you could write a program to predict whether a given passenger would survive the disaster. However, writing such a program in Python does not make much sense. Naturally, it would be very tedious to write, difficult to generalize, and would require extensive fine-tuning for each variable and samples (that is, each passenger):

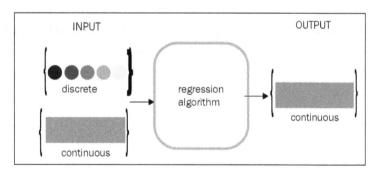

Figure 10: A regression algorithm is meant to produce continuous output

At this point, you might have confusion in your mind about what the basic difference between a classification and a regression problem is. Well, a regression algorithm is meant to produce continuous output. The input is allowed to be either discrete or continuous. In contrast, a classification algorithm is meant to produce discrete output from an input from a set of discrete or continuous values. This distinction is important to know because discrete-valued outputs are handled better by classification, which will be discussed in upcoming sections:

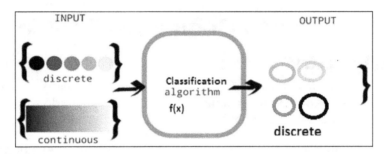

Figure 11: A classification algorithm is meant to produce discrete output

In this section, we will see how we could develop several predictive models for Titanic survival prediction and do some analytics using them. In particular, we will discuss logistic regression, random forest, and linear SVM. We start with logistic regression. Then we go with SVM since the number of features is not that large. Finally, we will see how we could improve the performance using Random Forests. However, before diving in too deeply, a short exploratory analysis of the dataset is required.

An Exploratory Analysis of the Titanic Dataset

We will see how the variables contribute to survival. At first, we need to import the required packages:

```
import os
import pandas as pd
import numpy as np
import seaborn as sns
import matplotlib.pyplot as plt
from sklearn.model_selection import train_test_split
from sklearn.metrics import classification_report
import shutil
```

Now, let's load the data and check what the features available to us are:

```
train = pd.read_csv(os.path.join('input', 'train.csv'))
test = pd.read_csv(os.path.join('input', 'test.csv'))
print("Information about the data")
print(train.info())
>>>
RangeIndex: 891 entries, 0 to 890
Data columns (total 12 columns):
PassengerId    891 non-null int64
Survived       891 non-null int64
Pclass         891 non-null int64
Name           891 non-null object
Sex            891 non-null object
Age            714 non-null float64
SibSp          891 non-null int64
Parch          891 non-null int64
Ticket         891 non-null object
Fare           891 non-null float64
Cabin          204 non-null object
Embarked       889 non-null object
```

So, the training dataset has 12 columns and 891 rows altogether. Also, the Age, Cabin, and Embarked columns have null or missing values. We will take care of the null values in the feature engineering section, but for the time being, let's see how many have survived:

```
print("How many have survived?")
print(train.Survived.value_counts(normalize=True))
count_plot = sns.countplot(train.Survived)
count_plot.get_figure().savefig("survived_count.png")
>>>
```

How many have survived?

```
0    0.616162
1    0.383838
```

So, approximately 61% died and only 39% of passengers managed to survive as shown in the following figure:

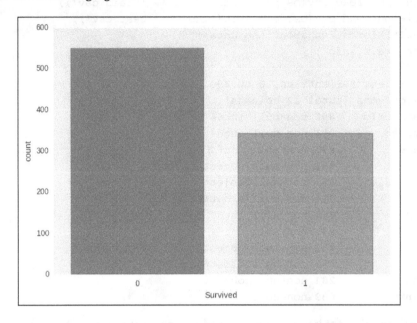

Figure 12: Survived versus dead from the Titanic training set

Now, what is the relationship between the class and the rate of survival? At first we should see the counts for each class:

```
train['Name_Title'] = train['Name'].apply(lambda x: x.split(',')[1]).
apply(lambda x: x.split()[0])
print('Title count')
print(train['Name_Title'].value_counts())
print('Survived by title')
print(train['Survived'].groupby(train['Name_Title']).mean())
>>>
Title       count
Mr.          517
Miss.        182
Mrs.         125
Master.       40
Dr.            7
Rev.           6
Mlle.          2
Col.           2
Major.         2
Sir.           1
```

```
Jonkheer.        1
Lady.            1
Capt.            1
the              1
Don.             1
Ms.              1
Mme.             1
```

As you may remember from the movie (that is, Titanic 1997), people from higher classes had better chances of surviving. So, you may assume that the title could be an important factor in survival, too. Another funny thing is that people with longer names have a higher probability of survival. This happens due to most of the people with longer names being married ladies whose husband or family members probably helped them to survive:

```
train['Name_Len'] = train['Name'].apply(lambda x: len(x))
print('Survived by name length')
print(train['Survived'].groupby(pd.qcut(train['Name_Len'],5)).mean())
>>>
Survived by name length
(11.999, 19.0]      0.220588
(19.0, 23.0]        0.301282
(23.0, 27.0]        0.319797
(27.0, 32.0]        0.442424
(32.0, 82.0]        0.674556
```

Women and children had a higher chance to survive, since they are the first to evacuate the shipwreck:

```
print('Survived by sex')
print(train['Survived'].groupby(train['Sex']).mean())
>>>
Survived by sex
Sex
female    0.742038
male      0.188908
```

Cabin has the most nulls (almost 700), but we can still extract information from it, like the first letter of each cabin. Therefore, we can see that most of the cabin letters are associated with survival rate:

```
train['Cabin_Letter'] = train['Cabin'].apply(lambda x: str(x)[0])
print('Survived by Cabin_Letter')
print(train['Survived'].groupby(train['Cabin_Letter']).mean())
>>>
Survived by Cabin_Letter
```

```
A    0.466667
B    0.744681
C    0.593220
D    0.757576
E    0.750000
F    0.615385
G    0.500000
T    0.000000
n    0.299854
```

Finally, it also seems that people who embarked at Cherbourg had a 20% higher survival rate than those embarked at other embarking locations. This is very likely due to the high percentage of upper-class passengers from that location:

```
print('Survived by Embarked')
print(train['Survived'].groupby(train['Embarked']).mean())
count_plot = sns.countplot(train['Embarked'], hue=train['Pclass'])
count_plot.get_figure().savefig("survived_count_by_embarked.png")

>>>
Survived by Embarked
C    0.553571
Q    0.389610
S    0.336957
```

Graphically, the preceding result can be seen as follows:

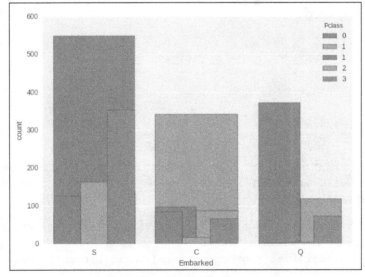

Figure 13: Survived by embarked

Thus, there were several important factors to people's survival. This means we need to consider these facts while developing our predictive models.

We will train several binary classifiers since this is a binary classification problem having two predictors, that is, 0 and 1 using the training set and will use the test set for making survival predictions.

But, before we even do that, let's do some feature engineering since you have seen that there are some missing or null values. We will either impute them or drop the entry from the training and test set. Moreover, we cannot use our datasets directly, but need to prepare them such that they could feed our machine learning models.

Feature Engineering

Since we are considering the length of the passenger's name as an important feature, it would be better to remove the name itself and compute the corresponding length and also we extract only the title:

def create_name_feat(train, test):

```
    for i in [train, test]:
        i['Name_Len'] = i['Name'].apply(lambda x: len(x))
        i['Name_Title'] = i['Name'].apply(lambda x: x.split(',')[1]).
apply(lambda x: x.split()[0])
        del i['Name']
    return train, test
```

As there are 177 null values for Age, and those ones have a 10% lower survival rate than the non-nulls. Therefore, before imputing values for the nulls, we are including an Age_null flag, just to make sure we can account for this characteristic of the data:

```
def age_impute(train, test):
    for i in [train, test]:
        i['Age_Null_Flag'] = i['Age'].apply(lambda x: 1 if
pd.isnull(x) else 0)
        data = train.groupby(['Name_Title', 'Pclass'])['Age']
        i['Age'] = data.transform(lambda x: x.fillna(x.mean()))
    return train, test
```

We are imputing the null age values with the mean of that column. This will add some extra bias in the dataset. But, for the betterment of our predictive model, we will have to sacrifice something.

Then we combine the SibSp and Parch columns to create get family size and break it into three levels:

```
def fam_size(train, test):
    for i in [train, test]:
        i['Fam_Size'] = np.where((i['SibSp']+i['Parch']) == 0, 'One',
                            np.where((i['SibSp']+i['Parch']) <=
3, 'Small', 'Big'))
        del i['SibSp']
        del i['Parch']
    return train, test
```

We are using the Ticket column to create Ticket_Letr, which indicates the first letter of each ticket and Ticket_Len, which indicates the length of the Ticket field:

```
def ticket_grouped(train, test):
    for i in [train, test]:
        i['Ticket_Letr'] = i['Ticket'].apply(lambda x: str(x)[0])
        i['Ticket_Letr'] = i['Ticket_Letr'].apply(lambda x: str(x))
        i['Ticket_Letr'] = np.where((i['Ticket_Letr']).isin(['1', '2',
'3', 'S', 'P', 'C', 'A']),
                                i['Ticket_Letr'],
                                np.where((i['Ticket_Letr']).
isin(['W', '4', '7', '6', 'L', '5', '8']),'Low_ticket', 'Other_
ticket'))
        i['Ticket_Len'] = i['Ticket'].apply(lambda x: len(x))
        del i['Ticket']
    return train, test
```

We also need to extract the first letter of the Cabin column:

```
def cabin(train, test):
    for i in [train, test]:
        i['Cabin_Letter'] = i['Cabin'].apply(lambda x: str(x)[0])
        del i['Cabin']
    return train, test
```

Fill the null values in the Embarked column with the most commonly occurring value, which is 'S':

```
def embarked_impute(train, test):
    for i in [train, test]:
        i['Embarked'] = i['Embarked'].fillna('S')
    return train, test
```

We now need to convert our categorical columns. So far, we have considered it important for the predictive models that we will be creating to have numerical values for string variables. The `dummies()` function below does a one-hot encoding to the string variables:

```python
def dummies(train, test,
            columns = ['Pclass', 'Sex', 'Embarked', 'Ticket_Letr',
'Cabin_Letter', 'Name_Title', 'Fam_Size']):
    for column in columns:
        train[column] = train[column].apply(lambda x: str(x))
        test[column] = test[column].apply(lambda x: str(x))
        good_cols = [column+'_'+i for i in train[column].unique() if i
in test[column].unique()]
        train = pd.concat((train, pd.get_dummies(train[column],
prefix=column)[good_cols]), axis=1)
        test = pd.concat((test, pd.get_dummies(test[column],
prefix=column)[good_cols]), axis=1)
        del train[column]
        del test[column]
    return train, test
```

We have the numerical features, finally, we need to create a separate column for the predicted values or targets:

```python
def PrepareTarget(data):
    return np.array(data.Survived, dtype='int8').reshape(-1, 1)
```

We have seen the data and its characteristics and done some feature engineering to construct the best features for the linear models. The next task is to build the predictive models and make a prediction on the test set. Let's start with the logistic regression.

Logistic Regression for Survival Prediction

Logistic regression is one of the most widely used classifiers to predict a binary response. It is a linear machine learning method The `loss` function in the formulation given by the logistic loss:

$$L\left(\mathbf{w}; \mathbf{x}, y\right) := \log\left(1 + \exp\left(-y\mathbf{w}^{T}\mathbf{x}\right)\right)$$

For the logistic regression model, the loss function is the logistic loss. For a binary classification problem, the algorithm outputs a binary logistic regression model such that, for a given new data point, denoted by **x**, the model makes predictions by applying the logistic function:

$$f(z) = \frac{1}{1 + e^{-z}}$$

In the preceding equation, $z = W^T X$ **and** if $f(W^T X) > 0.5$, the outcome is positive; otherwise, it is negative. Note that the raw output of the logistic regression model, **f (z)**, has a probabilistic interpretation.

Well, if you now compare logistic regression with its predecessor linear regression, the former provides you with a higher accuracy of the classification result. Moreover, it is a flexible way to regularize a model for custom adjustment and overall the model responses are measures of probability. And, most importantly, whereas linear regression can predict only continuous values, logistic regression can be generalized enough to make it predict discrete values. From now on, we will often be using the TensorFlow contrib API. So let's have a quick look at it.

Using TensorFlow Contrib

The contrib is a high level API for learning with TensorFlow. It supports the following Estimators:

- `tf.contrib.learn.BaseEstimator`
- `tf.contrib.learn.Estimator`
- `tf.contrib.learn.Trainable`
- `tf.contrib.learn.Evaluable`
- `tf.contrib.learn.KMeansClustering`
- `tf.contrib.learn.ModeKeys`
- `tf.contrib.learn.ModelFnOps`
- `tf.contrib.learn.MetricSpec`
- `tf.contrib.learn.PredictionKey`
- `tf.contrib.learn.DNNClassifier`
- `tf.contrib.learn.DNNRegressor`
- `tf.contrib.learn.DNNLinearCombinedRegressor`
- `tf.contrib.learn.DNNLinearCombinedClassifier`

- `tf.contrib.learn.LinearClassifier`
- `tf.contrib.learn.LinearRegressor`
- `tf.contrib.learn.LogisticRegressor`

Thus, without developing the logistic regression, from scratch, we will use the estimator from the TensorFlow contrib package. When we are creating our own estimator from scratch, the constructor still accepts two high-level parameters for model configuration, `model_fn` and `params`:

```
nn = tf.contrib.learn.Estimator(model_fn=model_fn, params=model_
params)
```

To instantiate an Estimator we need to provide two parameters such as `model_fn` and the `model_params` as follows:

```
nn = tf.contrib.learn.Estimator(model_fn=model_fn, params=model_
params)
```

It is to be noted that the `model_fn()` function contains all the above mentioned TensorFlow logic to support the training, evaluation, and prediction. Thus, you only need to implement the functionality that could use it efficiently.

Now, upon invoking the `main()` method, `model_params` containing the learning rate, instantiates the Estimator. You can define the `model_params` as follows:

```
model_params = {"learning_rate": LEARNING_RATE}
```

 For more information on the TensorFlow contrib, interested readers can refer to this URL at `https://www.tensorflow.org/extend/estimators`

Well, so far we have acquired enough background knowledge to create an LR model with TensorFlow with our dataset. It's time to implement it:

1. Import required packages and modules:
   ```
   import os
   import shutil
   import random
   import pandas as pd
   import numpy as np
   import seaborn as sns
   import matplotlib.pyplot as plt
   from sklearn.model_selection import train_test_split
   from sklearn.metrics import classification_report
   from sklearn.metrics import confusion_matrix
   ```

```
from feature import *
import tensorflow as tf
from tensorflow.contrib.learn.python.learn.estimators import
estimator
from tensorflow.contrib import learn
```

2. Loading and preparing the dataset.

   At first, we load both the datasets:

```
random.seed(12345) # For the reproducibility
train = pd.read_csv(os.path.join('input', 'train.csv'))
test = pd.read_csv(os.path.join('input', 'test.csv'))
```

Let's do some feature engineering. We will invoke the function we defined in the feature engineering section, but will be provided as separate Python script with name `feature.py`:

```
train, test = create_name_feat(train, test)
train, test = age_impute(train, test)
train, test = cabin(train, test)
train, test = embarked_impute(train, test)
train, test = fam_size(train, test)
test['Fare'].fillna(train['Fare'].mean(), inplace=True)
train, test = ticket_grouped(train, test)
```

It is to be noted that the sequence of the above invocation is important to make the training and test set consistent. Now, we also need to create numerical values for categorical variables using the `dummies()` function from sklearn:

```
train, test = dummies(train, test, columns=['Pclass', 'Sex',
'Embarked', 'Ticket_Letr', 'Cabin_Letter', 'Name_Title', 'Fam_
Size'])
```

We need to prepare the training and test set:

```
TEST = True
if TEST:
    train, test = train_test_split(train, test_size=0.25, random_
state=10)
    train = train.sort_values('PassengerId')
    test = test.sort_values('PassengerId')

X_train = train.iloc[:, 1:]
x_test = test.iloc[:, 1:]
```

We then convert the training and test set into a NumPy array since so far we have kept them in Pandas DataFrame format:

```
x_train = np.array(x_train.iloc[:, 1:], dtype='float32')
if TEST:
    x_test = np.array(x_test.iloc[:, 1:], dtype='float32')
else:
    x_test = np.array(x_test, dtype='float32')
```

Let's prepare the target column for prediction:

```
y_train = PrepareTarget(train)
```

We also need to know the feature count to build the LR estimator:

```
feature_count = x_train.shape[1]
```

3. Preparing the LR estimator.

   We build the LR estimator. We will utilize the `LinearClassfier` estimator for it. Since this is a binary classification problem, we provide two classes:

```
def build_lr_estimator(model_dir, feature_count):
    return estimator.SKCompat(learn.LinearClassifier(
        feature_columns=[tf.contrib.layers.real_valued_column("",
dimension=feature_count)],
        n_classes=2, model_dir=model_dir))
```

4. Training the model.

   Here, we train the above LR estimator for `10,000` iterations. The `fit()` method does the trick and the `predict()` method computes the prediction on the training set containing the feature, that is, `x_train` and the label, that is, `y_train`:

```
print("Training...")
try:
    shutil.rmtree('lr/')
except OSError:
    pass
lr = build_lr_estimator('lr/', feature_count)
lr.fit(x_train, y_train, steps=1000)
lr_pred = lr.predict(x_test)
lr_pred = lr_pred['classes']
```

5. Model evaluation.

We will evaluate the model seeing several classification performance metrics such as precision, recall, f1 score, and confusion matrix:

```
if TEST:
    target_names = ['Not Survived', 'Survived']
    print("Logistic Regression Report")
    print(classification_report(test['Survived'], lr_pred,
target_names=target_names))
    print("Logistic Regression Confusion Matrix")
```

```
>>>
Logistic Regression Report
                  precision    recall  f1-score   support
Not Survived        0.90        0.88      0.89       147
Survived            0.78        0.80      0.79        76-------
--------------------------------------------------
 avg / total        0.86        0.86      0.86       223
```

Since we trained the LR model with NumPy data, we now need to convert it back to a Panda DataFrame for confusion matrix creation:

```
cm = confusion_matrix(test['Survived'], lr_pred)
    df_cm = pd.DataFrame(cm, index=[i for i in ['Not Survived',
'Survived']],
                      columns=[i for i in ['Not Survived',
'Survived']])
    print(df_cm)
```

```
>>>
Logistic Regression Confusion Matrix
              Not Survived  Survived
Not Survived           130        17
Survived                15        61
```

Now, let's see the count:

```
print("Predicted Counts")
print(sol.Survived.value_counts())
```

```
>>>
Predicted Counts
0    145
1     78
```

Since seeing the count graphically is awesome, let's draw it:

```
sol = pd.DataFrame()
sol['PassengerId'] = test['PassengerId']
sol['Survived'] = pd.Series(lr_pred.reshape(-1)).map({True:1,
False:0}).values
sns.plt.suptitle("Predicted Survived LR")
count_plot = sns.countplot(sol.Survived)
count_plot.get_figure().savefig("survived_count_lr_prd.png")


>>>
```

The output is as follows:

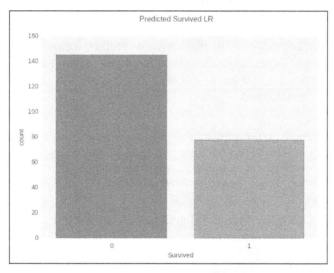

Figure 14: Survival prediction using logistic regression with TensorFlow

So, the accuracy we achieved with the LR model is 86% which is not that bad at all. But it can still be improved with better predictive models. In the next section, we will try to do that using linear **SVM** for survival prediction.

Linear SVM for Survival Prediction

The linear **SVM** is one of the most widely used and standard methods for large-scale classification tasks. Both the multiclass and binary classification problem can be solved using SVM with the loss function in the formulation given by the hinge loss:

$$L(w; x, y) := \max\{0, 1 - yw^T x\}$$

Usually, linear SVMs are trained with L2 regularization. Eventually, the linear SVM algorithm outputs an SVM model that can be used to predict the label of unknown data.

Suppose you have an unknown data point, **x**, the SVM model makes predictions based on the value of $W^T X$. The outcome can be either positive or negative. More specifically, if $W^T X \geq 0$, then the predicted value is positive; otherwise, it is negative.

The current version of the TensorFlow contrib package supports only the linear SVM. TensorFlow uses SDCAOptimizer for the underlying optimization. Now, the thing is that if you want to build an SVM model of your own, you need to consider the performance and convergence tuning issues. Fortunately, you can pass the `num_loss_partitions` parameter to the SDCAOptimizer function. But you need to set the **X** such that it converges to the concurrent train ops per worker.

If you set the `num_loss_partitions` larger than or equal to this value, convergence is guaranteed, but this makes the overall training slower with the increase of `num_loss_partitions`. On the other hand, if you set its value to a smaller one, the optimizer is more aggressive in reducing the global loss, but convergence is not guaranteed.

For more on the implemented contrib packages, interested readers should refer to this URL at `https://github.com/tensorflow/tensorflow/tree/master/tensorflow/contrib/learn/python/learn/estimators`.

Well, so far we have acquired enough background knowledge for creating an SVM model, now it's time to implement it:

1. Import the required packages and modules:

```
import os
import shutil
import random
import pandas as pd
import seaborn as sns
import matplotlib.pyplot as plt
from sklearn.model_selection import train_test_split
from sklearn.metrics import classification_report
from sklearn.metrics import confusion_matrix
from feature import *
import tensorflow as tf
from tensorflow.contrib.learn.python.learn.estimators import svm
```

2. Dataset preparation for building SVM model:

Now, the data preparation for building an SVM model is more or less the same as an LR model, except that we need to convert the `PassengerId` to string which is required for the SVM:

```
train['PassengerId'] = train['PassengerId'].astype(str)
test['PassengerId'] = test['PassengerId'].astype(str)
```

3. Creating a dictionary for SVM for continuous feature column.

> To feed the data to the SVM model, we further need to create a dictionary mapping from each continuous feature column name (k) to the values of that column stored in a constant Tensor. For more information on this issue, refer to this issue on TensorFlow GitHub repository at `https://github.com/tensorflow/tensorflow/issues/9505`.

I have written two functions for both the feature and labels. Let's see what the first one looks like:

```
def train_input_fn():
    continuous_cols = {k: tf.expand_dims(tf.constant(train[k].
values), 1)
                       for k in list(train) if k not in
['Survived', 'PassengerId']}
    id_col = {'PassengerId' : tf.constant(train['PassengerId'].
values)}
    feature_cols = continuous_cols.copy()
    feature_cols.update(id_col)
    label = tf.constant(train["Survived"].values)
    return feature_cols, label
```

The preceding function creates a dictionary mapping from each continuous feature column and then another for the `passengerId` column. Then I merged them into one. Since we want to target the 'Survived' column as the labels, I converted the label column into constant tensor. Finally, through this function, I returned both the feature column and the label.

Now, the second method does almost the same trick except that it returns only the feature columns as follows:

```
def predict_input_fn():
    continuous_cols = {k: tf.expand_dims(tf.constant(test[k].
values), 1)
                       for k in list(test) if k not in
['Survived', 'PassengerId']}
    id_col = {'PassengerId' : tf.constant(test['PassengerId'].
```

```
values)}
    feature_cols = continuous_cols.copy()
    feature_cols.update(id_col)
    return feature_cols
```

4. Training the SVM model.

    Now we will iterate the training 10,000 times over the real valued column only. Finally, it creates a prediction list containing all the prediction values:

```
svm_model = svm.SVM(example_id_column="PassengerId",
                    feature_columns=[tf.contrib.layers.real_
valued_column(k) for k in list(train)
                                    if k not in ['Survived',
'PassengerId']],
                    model_dir="svm/")
svm_model.fit(input_fn=train_input_fn, steps=10000)
svm_pred = list(svm_model.predict_classes(input_fn=predict_input_
fn))
```

5. Evaluation of the model:

```
target_names = ['Not Survived', 'Survived']
print("SVM Report")
print(classification_report(test['Survived'], svm_pred, target_
names=target_names))
>>>
SVM Report
                     precision    recall  f1-score   support
Not Survived            0.94        0.72      0.82       117
Survived                0.63        0.92      0.75        62-----------
          -----------------------------------------
  avg / total           0.84        0.79      0.79       179
```

Thus using SVM, the accuracy is only 79%, which is lower than that of an LR model. Well, similar to an LR model, draw and observe the confusion matrix:

```
print("SVM Confusion Matrix")
cm = confusion_matrix(test['Survived'], svm_pred)
df_cm = pd.DataFrame(cm, index=[i for i in ['Not Survived',
'Survived']],
                     columns=[i for i in ['Not Survived',
'Survived']])
print(df_cm)
>>>
SVM Confusion Matrix
          Not Survived  Survived
```

```
Not Survived           84          33
Survived                5          57
```

Then, let's draw the count plot to see the ratio visually:

```
sol = pd.DataFrame()
sol['PassengerId'] = test['PassengerId']
sol['Survived'] = pd.Series(svm_pred).values
sns.plt.suptitle("Titanic Survival prediction using SVM with
TensorFlow")
count_plot = sns.countplot(sol.Survived)
```

The output is as follows:

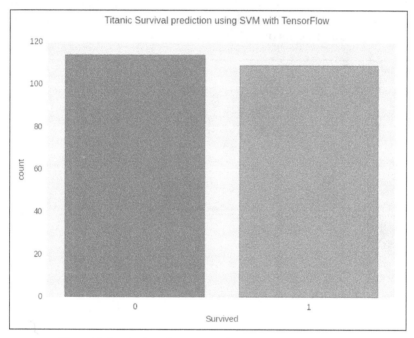

Figure 15: Survival prediction using linear SVM with TensorFlow

Now, the count:

```
print("Predicted Counts")
print(sol.Survived.value_counts())

>>>
Predicted Counts
1    90
0    89
```

Ensemble Method for Survival Prediction – Random Forest

One of the most widely used machine learning techniques is using the ensemble methods, which are learning algorithms that construct a set of classifiers. It can then be used to classify new data points by taking a weighted vote of their predictions. In this section, we will mainly focus on the random forest that can be built by combining 100s of decision trees.

Decision trees (DTs) is a technique which is used in supervised learning for solving classification and regression tasks. Where a DT model learns simple decision rules that are inferred from the data features by utilizing a tree-like graph to demonstrate the course of actions. Each branch of a decision tree represents a possible decision, occurrence or reaction in terms of statistical probability:

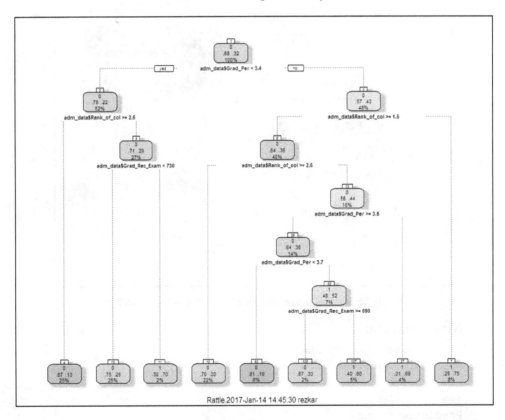

Figure 16: A sample decision tree on the admission test dataset using the rattle package of R

Compared to LR or SVM, the DTs are far more robust classification algorithms. The tree infers predicted labels or classes after splitting available features to the training data based to produce a good generalization. Most interestingly, the algorithm can handle both the binary as well as multiclass classification problems.

For instance, the decision trees in figure 16 learn from the admission data to approximate a sine curve with a set of `if...else` decision rules. The dataset contains the record of each student who applied for admission, say to an American university. Each record contains the graduate record exam score, CGPA score and the rank of the column. Now we will have to predict who is competent based on these three features (variables).

DTs can be utilized to solve this kind of problem after training the DT model and pruning the unwanted branch of the tree. In general, a deeper tree signifies more complex decision rules and a better-fitted model. Therefore, the deeper the tree, the more complex the decision rules, and the more fitted the model.

 If you would like to draw the above figure, just use my R script and execute on RStudio and feed the admission dataset. The script and the dataset can be found in my GitHub repository at `https://github.com/rezacsedu/AdmissionUsingDecisionTree`.

Well, so far we have acquired enough background knowledge for creating a Random Forest (RF) model, now it's time to implement it.

1. Import the required packages and modules:

```
import os
import shutil
import random
import pandas as pd
import numpy as np
import seaborn as sns
import matplotlib.pyplot as plt
from sklearn.model_selection import train_test_split
from sklearn.metrics import classification_report
from sklearn.metrics import confusion_matrix
from feature import *
import tensorflow as tf
from tensorflow.contrib.learn.python.learn.estimators import
estimator
from tensorflow.contrib.tensor_forest.client import random_forest
from tensorflow.contrib.tensor_forest.python import tensor_forest
```

2. Dataset preparation for building an RF model.

   Now, the data preparation for building an RF model is more or less the same as an LR model. So please refer to the logistic regression section.

3. Building a random forest estimator.

   The following function builds a random forest estimator. It creates 1,000 trees with maximum 1,000 nodes and 10-fold cross-validation. Since it's a binary classification problem, I put number of classes as 2:

```
def build_rf_estimator(model_dir, feature_count):
    params = tensor_forest.ForestHParams(
        num_classes=2,
        num_features=feature_count,
        num_trees=1000,
        max_nodes=1000,
        min_split_samples=10)
    graph_builder_class = tensor_forest.RandomForestGraphs
    return estimator.SKCompat(random_forest.TensorForestEstimator(
        params, graph_builder_class=graph_builder_class,
        model_dir=model_dir))
```

4. Training the RF model.

   Here, we train the above RF estimator. Once the `fit()` method does the trick and the `predict()` method computes the prediction on the training set containing the feature, that is, `x_train` and the label, that is, `y_train`:

```
rf = build_rf_estimator('rf/', feature_count)
rf.fit(x_train, y_train, batch_size=100)
rf_pred = rf.predict(x_test)
rf_pred = rf_pred['classes']
```

5. Evaluating the model.

   Now let's evaluate the performance of the RF model:

```
    target_names = ['Not Survived', 'Survived']
    print("RandomForest Report")
    print(classification_report(test['Survived'], rf_pred, target_
names=target_names))


    >>>
```

```
RandomForest Report
                        precision   recall  f1-score   support
------------------------------------------------------------
Not Survived     0.92         0.85       0.88         117
Survived         0.76         0.85       0.80          62
------------------------------------------------------------
avg / total      0.86         0.85       0.86         179
```

Thus, using RF, the accuracy is 87% which is higher than that of the LR and SVM models. Well, similar to the LR and SVM model, we'll draw and observe the confusion matrix:

```
    print("Random Forest Confusion Matrix")
    cm = confusion_matrix(test['Survived'], rf_pred)
    df_cm = pd.DataFrame(cm, index=[i for i in ['Not Survived',
'Survived']],
                         columns=[i for i in ['Not Survived',
'Survived']])
    print(df_cm)
>>>
Random Forest Confusion Matrix
                      Not Survived  Survived
------------------------------------------------------------
Not Survived            100            17
Survived                  9            53
```

Then, let's draw the count plot to see the ratio visually:

```
sol = pd.DataFrame()
sol['PassengerId'] = test['PassengerId']
sol['Survived'] = pd.Series(svm_pred).values
sns.plt.suptitle("Titanic Survival prediction using RF with
TensorFlow")
count_plot = sns.countplot(sol.Survived)
```

The output is as follows:

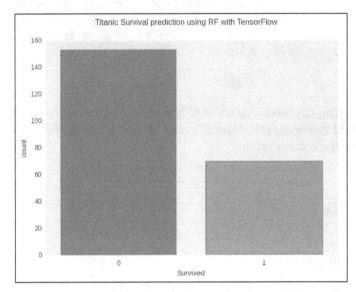

Figure 17: Titanic survival prediction using random forest with TensorFlow

Now, the count for each one:

```
print("Predicted Counts")
print(sol.Survived.value_counts())
>>>   Predicted Counts
--------------------------
0    109
1     70
```

A Comparative Analysis

From the classification reports, we can see that random forest has the best overall performance. The reason for this may be that it works better with categorical features than the other two methods. Also, since it uses implicit feature selection, overfitting was reduced significantly. Using logistic regression is a convenient probability score for observations. However, it doesn't perform well when feature space is too large that is, doesn't handle a large number of categorical features/variables well. It also solely relies on transformations for non-linear features.

Finally, using SVM we can handle a large feature space with non-linear feature interactions without relying on the entire dataset. However, it is not very well with a large number of observations. Nevertheless, it can be tricky to find an appropriate kernel sometimes.

Summary

In this lesson, we have discussed supervised learning from the theoretical and practical perspective. In particular, we have revisited the linear regression model for regression analysis. We have seen how to use regression for predicting continuous values. Later in this lesson, we have discussed some other supervised learning algorithms for predictive analytics. We have seen how to use logistic regression, SVM, and random forests for survival prediction on the Titanic dataset. Finally, we have seen a comparative analysis between these classifiers. We have also seen that random forest, which is based on decision trees ensembles, outperforms logistic regression and linear SVM models.

In *Lesson 3*, *Clustering Your Data – Unsupervised Learning for Predictive Analytics*, we will provide some practical examples of unsupervised learning. Particularly, the clustering technique using TensorFlow will be provided for neighborhood clustering and audio clustering from audio features.

More specifically, we will provide an exploratory analysis of the dataset then we will develop a cluster of the neighborhood using K-means, K-NN, and bisecting K-means with sufficient performance metrics such as cluster cost, accuracy, and so on. In the second part of the lesson, we will see how to do audio feature clustering. Finally, we will provide a comparative analysis of clustering algorithms.

Assessments

1. Depending on the nature of the learning feedback available, the machine learning process is typically classified into three broad categories. Name them.

2. State whether the following statement is True or False: Using the brute-force approach such as if-else statements with some sort of weighted scoring system, you cannot write a program to predict whether a given passenger would survive the disaster.

3. Upon invoking the main() method, model_params containing the learning rate instantiates the Estimator. How can you define the model_params as?

4. State whether the following statement is True or False: Each branch of a decision tree represents a possible decision, occurrence, or reaction in terms of statistical probability.

5. A predictive model based on supervised learning algorithms can make predictions based on a labeled _____ that maps inputs to outputs aligning with the real world.

    1. Dataflow graph
    2. Linear graph
    3. Regression model
    4. Dataset

3
Clustering Your Data – Unsupervised Learning for Predictive Analytics

In this lesson, we will dig deeper into predictive analytics and find out how we can take advantage of it to cluster records belonging to a certain group or class for a dataset of unsupervised observations. We will provide some practical examples of unsupervised learning; in particular, clustering techniques using TensorFlow will be discussed with some hands-on examples.

The following topics will be covered in this lesson:

- Unsupervised learning and clustering
- Using K-means for predicting neighborhood
- Using K-means for clustering audio files
- Using unsupervised **k-nearest neighborhood (kNN)** for predicting nearest neighbors

Unsupervised Learning and Clustering

In this section, we will provide a brief introduction to the unsupervised **machine learning (ML)** technique. Unsupervised learning is a type of ML algorithm used for grouping related data objects and finding hidden patterns by inferencing from unlabeled datasets, that is, a training set consisting of input data without labels.

Let's see a real-life example. Suppose you have a large collection of not-pirated-totally-legal MP3s in a crowded and massive folder on your hard drive. Now, what if you can build a predictive model that helps automatically group together similar songs and organize them into your favorite categories such as country, rap, and rock?

This is an act of assigning an item to a group so that an MP3 is added to the respective playlist in an unsupervised way. In *Lesson 1, From Data to Decisions – Getting Started with TensorFlow, on classification*, we assumed that you're given a training dataset of correctly labeled data. Unfortunately, we don't always have that extravagance when we collect data in the real world. For example, suppose we would like to divide a huge collection of music into interesting playlists. How can we possibly group together songs if we don't have direct access to their metadata? One possible approach is a mixture of various ML techniques, but clustering is often at the heart of the solution.

In other words, the main objective of the unsupervised learning algorithms is to explore the unknown/hidden patterns in the input data that are unlabeled. Unsupervised learning, however, also comprehends other techniques to explain the key features of the data in an exploratory way toward finding the hidden patterns. To overcome this challenge, clustering techniques are used widely to group unlabeled data points based on certain similarity measures in an unsupervised way.

In a clustering task, an algorithm groups related features into categories by analyzing similarities between input examples, where similar features are clustered and marked using circles.

Clustering uses include but are not limited to the following points:

- Anomaly detection for suspicious pattern finding in an unsupervised way
- Text categorization for finding useful patterns in the tests for NLP
- Social network analysis for finding coherent groups
- Data center computing clusters for finding a way of putting related computers together
- Real estate data analysis for identifying neighborhoods based on similar features

Clustering analysis is about dividing data samples or data points and putting them into corresponding homogeneous classes or clusters. Thus, a trivial definition of clustering can be thought of as the process of organizing objects into groups whose members are similar in some way, as shown in figure 1:

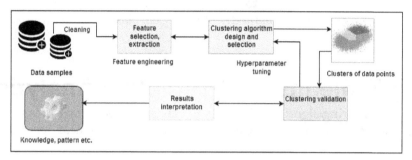

Figure 1: A typical data pipelines for clustering raw data

A cluster is, therefore, a collection of objects that have a similarity between them and are dissimilar to the objects belonging to other clusters. If a collection of objects is provided, clustering algorithms put these objects into groups based on similarity. For example, a clustering algorithm such as K-means locates the centroid of the groups of data points.

However, to make clustering accurate and effective, the algorithm evaluates the distance between each point from the centroid of the cluster. Eventually, the goal of clustering is to determine intrinsic grouping in a set of unlabeled data. For example, the K-means algorithm tries to cluster related data points within the predefined 3 (that is $k = 3$) clusters, as shown in figure 2:

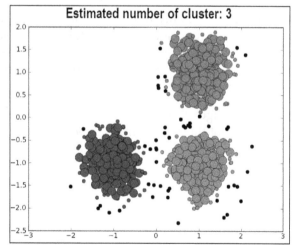

Figure 2: The results of a typical clustering algorithm and a representation of the cluster centers

Clustering is a process of intelligently categorizing items in your dataset. The overall idea is that two items in the same cluster are closer to each other than items that belong to separate clusters. This is a general definition, leaving the interpretation of closeness open. For example, perhaps cheetahs and leopards belong to the same cluster, whereas elephants belong to another when closeness is measured by the similarity of two species in the hierarchy of biological classification (family, genus, and species).

Using K-means for Predictive Analytics

K-means is a clustering algorithm that tries to cluster related data points together. However, we should know its working principle and mathematical operations.

How K-means Works

Suppose we have n data points, xi, $i = 1...n$, that need to be partitioned into k clusters. Now that the target here is to assign a cluster to each data point, K-means aims to find the positions, μi, $i=1...k$, of the clusters that minimize the distance from the data points to the cluster. Mathematically, the K-means algorithm tries to achieve the goal by solving an equation that is an optimization problem:

$$\arg\min_{c} \sum_{i=1}^{k} \sum_{\mathbf{x} \in c_i} d(\mathbf{x}, \mu_i) = \arg\min_{c} \sum_{i=1}^{k} \sum_{\mathbf{x} \in c_i} \|\mathbf{x} - \mu_i\|_2^2$$

In the previous equation, $\mathbf{c}i$ is a set of data points, which when assigned to cluster $\mathbf{i}$ and $d(\mathbf{x}, \mu_i) = \|\mathbf{x} - \mu_i\|_2^2$ is the Euclidean distance to be calculated (we will explain why we should use this distance measurement shortly). Therefore, we can see that the overall clustering operation using K-means is not a trivial one, but a NP-hard optimization problem. This also means that the K-means algorithm not only tries to find the global minima but often gets stuck in different solutions.

Clustering using the K-means algorithm begins by initializing all the coordinates to the centroids. With every pass of the algorithm, each point is assigned to its nearest centroid based on some distance metric, usually the Euclidean distance stated earlier.

Distance calculation: There are other ways to calculate the distance as well. For example, the Chebyshev distance can be used to measure the distance by considering only the most notable dimensions. The Hamming distance algorithm can identify the difference between two strings. Mahalanobis distance can be used to normalize the covariance matrix. The Manhattan distance is used to measure the distance by considering only axis-aligned directions. The Haversine distance is used to measure the great-circle distances between two points on a sphere from the location.

Considering these distance-measuring algorithms, it is clear that the Euclidean distance algorithm would be the most appropriate to solve our purpose of distance calculation in the K-means algorithm. The centroids are then updated to be the centers of all the points assigned to it in that iteration. This repeats until there is a minimal change in the centers. In short, the K-means algorithm is an iterative algorithm and works in two steps:

1. **Cluster assignment step**: K-means goes through each of the n data points in the dataset that is assigned to a cluster closest to the k centroids, then the least distant one is picked.

2. **Update step**: For each cluster, a new centroid is calculated for all the data points in the cluster. The overall workflow of K-means can be explained using a flowchart, as follows:

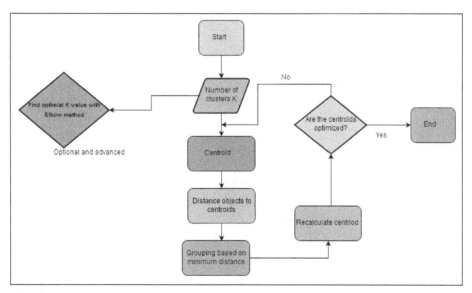

Figure 4: Flowchart of the K-means algorithm (Elbow method is an optional but also an advanced option)

Using K-means for Predicting Neighborhoods

Now, to show an example of clustering using K-means, we will use the Saratoga NY Homes dataset downloaded from `http://course1.winona.edu/bdeppa/Stat%20 425/Datasets.html` as an unsupervised learning technique. The dataset contains several features of the houses located in the suburb of the New York City; for example, price, lot size, waterfront, age, land value, new construct, central air, fuel type, heat type, sewer type, living area, Pct.College, bedrooms, fireplaces, bathrooms, and the number of rooms. However, only a few features have been shown in **Table 1**:

Price	Lot size	Water front	Age	Land value	Rooms
132500	0.09	0	42	5000	5
181115	0.92	0	0	22300	6
109000	0.19	0	133	7300	8
155000	0.41	0	13	18700	5
86060	0.11	0	0	15000	3
120000	0.68	0	31	14000	8
153000	0.4	0	33	23300	8
170000	1.21	0	23	146000	9
90000	0.83	0	36	222000	8
122900	1.94	0	4	212000	6
325000	2.29	0	123	126000	12

Table 1: A sample data from the Saratoga NY Homes dataset

The target of this clustering technique is to show an exploratory analysis based on the features of each house in the city for finding possible neighborhoods' of the house located in the same area. Before performing the feature extraction, we need to load and parse the Saratoga NY Homes dataset. However, we will look at this example with step-by-step source codes for better understanding:

1. Loading required libraries and packages.

    We need some built-in Python libraries, such as os, random, NumPy, and Pandas, for data manipulation; PCA for dimensionality reduction; Matplotlib for plotting; and of course, TensorFlow:

    ```
    import os
    import random
    from random import choice, shuffle
    import pandas as pd
    import numpy as np
    ```

```
import tensorflow as tf
from sklearn.decomposition import PCA
import matplotlib.pyplot as plt
from mpl_toolkits.mplot3d import axes3d, Axes3D
```

2. Loading, parsing, and preparing a training set.

   Here, the first line is used to ensure the reproducibility of the result. The second line basically reads the dataset from your location and converts it into the Pandas data frame:

```
random.seed(12345)
train = pd.read_csv(os.path.join('input', 'saratoga.csv'))
x_train = np.array(train.iloc[:, 1:], dtype='float32')
```

   If you now print the data frame (using print(train)), you should find the dataframe containing headers and data as shown in figure 3:

Price	LotSize	Waterfront	Age	LandValue	NewConstruct	CentralAir	FuelType	HeatType	SewerType	LivingArea	PctCollege	Bedrooms	Fireplaces	Bathrooms	rooms
132500.0	0.09	0.0	42.0	50000.0	0.0	0.0	3.0	4.0	2.0	906.0	35.0	2.0	1.0	1.0	5.0
181115.0	0.92	0.0	0.0	22300.0	0.0	0.0	2.0	3.0	2.0	1953.0	51.0	3.0	0.0	2.5	6.0
109000.0	0.19	0.0	133.0	7300.0	0.0	0.0	2.0	3.0	3.0	1944.0	51.0	4.0	1.0	1.0	8.0
155000.0	0.41	0.0	13.0	18700.0	0.0	0.0	2.0	2.0	2.0	1944.0	51.0	3.0	1.0	1.5	5.0
86060.0	0.11	0.0	0.0	15000.0	1.0	1.0	2.0	2.0	3.0	840.0	51.0	2.0	0.0	1.0	3.0
120000.0	0.68	0.0	31.0	14000.0	0.0	0.0	2.0	2.0	2.0	1152.0	22.0	4.0	1.0	1.0	8.0
153000.0	0.4	0.0	33.0	23300.0	0.0	0.0	4.0	3.0	2.0	2752.0	51.0	4.0	1.0	1.5	8.0
170000.0	1.21	0.0	23.0	14600.0	0.0	0.0	4.0	2.0	2.0	1662.0	35.0	4.0	1.0	1.5	9.0
90000.0	0.83	0.0	36.0	22200.0	0.0	0.0	3.0	4.0	2.0	1632.0	51.0	3.0	0.0	1.5	8.0
122900.0	1.94	0.0	4.0	21200.0	0.0	0.0	2.0	2.0	1.0	1416.0	44.0	3.0	0.0	1.5	6.0
325000.0	2.29	0.0	123.0	12600.0	0.0	0.0	4.0	2.0	2.0	2894.0	51.0	7.0	0.0	1.0	12.0
120000.0	0.92	0.0	1.0	22300.0	0.0	0.0	2.0	2.0	2.0	1624.0	51.0	3.0	0.0	2.0	6.0
85860.0	8.97	0.0	13.0	4800.0	0.0	0.0	3.0	4.0	2.0	704.0	41.0	2.0	0.0	1.0	4.0
97000.0	0.11	0.0	153.0	3100.0	0.0	0.0	2.0	3.0	3.0	1383.0	57.0	3.0	0.0	2.0	5.0
127000.0	0.14	0.0	9.0	300.0	0.0	0.0	4.0	2.0	2.0	1300.0	41.0	3.0	0.0	1.5	8.0
89900.0	0.0	0.0	88.0	2500.0	0.0	0.0	2.0	3.0	3.0	936.0	57.0	3.0	0.0	1.0	4.0
155000.0	0.13	0.0	9.0	300.0	0.0	0.0	4.0	2.0	2.0	1300.0	41.0	3.0	0.0	1.5	7.0
253750.0	2.0	0.0	0.0	49800.0	0.0	1.0	2.0	2.0	1.0	2816.0	71.0	4.0	1.0	2.5	12.0
60000.0	0.21	0.0	82.0	8500.0	0.0	0.0	4.0	3.0	2.0	924.0	35.0	2.0	0.0	1.0	6.0
87500.0	0.88	0.0	17.0	19400.0	0.0	0.0	4.0	2.0	2.0	1092.0	35.0	3.0	0.0	1.0	6.0

only showing top 20 rows

Figure 5: A snapshot of the Saratoga NY Homes dataset

   Well, we have managed to prepare the dataset. Now, the next task is to conceptualize our K-means and write a function/class for it.

3. Implementing K-means.

   The following is the source code of K-means, which is simple in a TensorFlow way:

```
def kmeans(x, n_features, n_clusters, n_max_steps=1000, early_
stop=0.0):
    input_vec = tf.constant(x, dtype=tf.float32)
    centroids = tf.Variable(tf.slice(tf.random_shuffle(input_vec),
[0, 0], [n_clusters, -1]), dtype=tf.float32)
    old_centroids = tf.Variable(tf.zeros([n_clusters, n_
features]), dtype=tf.float32)
    centroid_distance = tf.Variable(tf.zeros([n_clusters, n_
features]))
```

```
    expanded_vectors = tf.expand_dims(input_vec, 0)
    exanded_centroids = tf.expand_dims(centroids, 1)
    distances = tf.reduce_sum(tf.square(tf.subtract(expanded_
vectors, expanded_centroids)), 2)
    assignments = tf.argmin(distances, 0)
    means = tf.concat([tf.reduce_mean(
        tf.gather(input_vec, tf.reshape(tf.where(tf.
equal(assignments, c)), [1, -1])),
        reduction_indices=[1]) for c in range(n_clusters)], 0)
    save_old_centroids = tf.assign(old_centroids, centroids)
    update_centroids = tf.assign(centroids, means)
    init_op = tf.global_variables_initializer()
    performance = tf.assign(centroid_distance,
tf.subtract(centroids, old_centroids))
    check_stop = tf.reduce_sum(tf.abs(performance))
    with tf.Session() as sess:
        sess.run(init_op)
        for step in range(n_max_steps):
            sess.run(save_old_centroids)
            _, centroid_values, assignment_values = sess.run(
                [update_centroids, centroids, assignments])
            sess.run(check_stop)
            current_stop_coeficient = check_stop.eval()
            if current_stop_coeficient <= early_stop:
                break
    return centroid_values, assignment_values
```

The previous code contains all the steps required to develop the K-means model, including the distance-based centroid calculation, centroid update, and training parameters required.

4. Clustering the houses.

    Now the previous function can be invoked with real values, for example, our housing dataset. Since there are many houses with their respective features, it would be difficult to plot the clusters along with all the properties. This is the **Principal Component Analysis (PCA)** that we discussed in the previous lessons:

```
centers, cluster_assignments = kmeans(x_train, len(x_train[0]),
10)
pca_model = PCA(n_components=3)
reduced_data = pca_model.fit_transform(x_train)
reduced_centers = pca_model.transform(centers)
```

Well, now we are all set. It would be even better to visualize the clusters as shown in figure 6. For this, we will use mpl_toolkits.mplot3d for 3D projection, as follows:

```
plt.subplot(212, projection='3d')
plt.scatter(reduced_data[:, 0], reduced_data[:, 1], reduced_data[:, 2], c=cluster_assignments)
plt.title("Clusters")
plt.show()
>>>
```

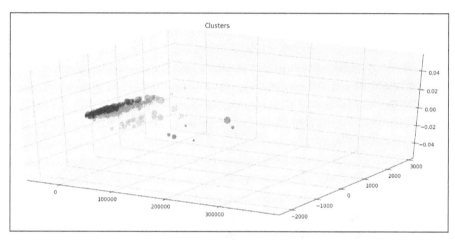

Figure 6: Clustering the houses with similar properties, for example, price

Here, we can see that most houses fall in **0** to **100,000** range. The second highest houses fall in the range of **100000** to **200000**. However, it's really difficult to separate them. Moreover, the number of predefined clusters that we used is 10, which might not be the most optimal one. Therefore, we need to tune this parameter.

5. Fine tuning and finding the optimal number of clusters.

    Choosing the right number of clusters often depends on the task. For example, suppose you're planning an event for hundreds of people, both young and old. If you have a budget for only two entertainment options, then you can use the K-means clustering with **k = 2** to separate the guests into two age groups. Other times, it's not as obvious what the value of k should be. Automatically figuring out the value of k is a bit more complicated.

    As mentioned earlier, the K-means algorithm tries to minimize the sum of squares of the distance (that is, Euclidean distance), in terms of **Within-Cluster Sum of Squares (WCSS)**.

However, if you want to minimize the sum of squares of the distance between the points of each set manually or automatically, you would end up with a model where each cluster is its own cluster center; in this case, this measure would be 0, but it would hardly be a generic enough model.

Therefore, once you have trained your model by specifying the parameters, you can evaluate the result using WCSS. Technically, it is same as the sum of distances of each observation in each K cluster. The beauty of clustering algorithms as a K-means algorithm is that it does the clustering on the data with an unlimited number of features. It is a great tool to use when you have raw data and would like to know the patterns in that data.

However, deciding the number of clusters prior to conducting the experiment might not be successful but sometimes may lead to an overfitting problem or an under-fitting one. Also, informally, determining the number of clusters is a separate but an optimization problem to be solved. So, based on this, we can redesign our K-means considering the WCSS value computation, as follows:

```
def kmeans(x, n_features, n_clusters, n_max_steps=1000, early_
stop=0.0):
    input_vec = tf.constant(x, dtype=tf.float32)
    centroids = tf.Variable(tf.slice(tf.random_shuffle(input_vec),
[0, 0], [n_clusters, -1]), dtype=tf.float32)
    old_centroids = tf.Variable(tf.zeros([n_clusters, n_
features]), dtype=tf.float32)
    centroid_distance = tf.Variable(tf.zeros([n_clusters, n_
features]))
    expanded_vectors = tf.expand_dims(input_vec, 0)
    expanded_centroids = tf.expand_dims(centroids, 1)
    distances = tf.reduce_sum(tf.square(tf.subtract(expanded_
vectors, expanded_centroids)), 2)
    assignments = tf.argmin(distances, 0)
    means = tf.concat([tf.reduce_mean(        tf.gather(input_vec,
tf.reshape(tf.where(tf.equal(assignments, c)), [1, -1])),
        reduction_indices=[1]) for c in range(n_clusters)], 0)
    save_old_centroids = tf.assign(old_centroids, centroids)
    update_centroids = tf.assign(centroids, means)
    init_op = tf.global_variables_initializer()

    performance = tf.assign(centroid_distance,
tf.subtract(centroids, old_centroids))
    check_stop = tf.reduce_sum(tf.abs(performance))
    calc_wss = tf.reduce_sum(tf.reduce_min(distances, 0))
```

```
with tf.Session() as sess:
    sess.run(init_op)
    for step in range(n_max_steps):
        sess.run(save_old_centroids)
        _, centroid_values, assignment_values = sess.run(
            [update_centroids, centroids, assignments])
        sess.run(calc_wss)
        sess.run(check_stop)
        current_stop_coeficient = check_stop.eval()
        wss = calc_wss.eval()
        print(step, current_stop_coeficient)
        if current_stop_coeficient <= early_stop:
            break
    return centroid_values, assignment_values, wss
```

To fine tune the clustering performance, we can use a heuristic approach called Elbow method. We start from **K = 2**. Then, we run the K-means algorithm by increasing K and observe the value of the cost function (CF) using WCSS. At some point, we should experience a big drop with respect to CF. Nevertheless, the improvement then becomes marginal with an increasing value of K.

In summary, we can pick the K after the last big drop of WCSS as the optimal one. The K-means includes various parameters such as withiness and betweenness, analyzing which you can find out the performance of K-means:

- ° **Betweenness**: This is the between sum of squares, also called the intra-cluster similarity

- ° **Withiness**: This is the within sum of squares, also called the inter-cluster similarity

- ° **Totwithiness**: This is the sum of all the withiness of all the clusters, also called the total intra-cluster similarity

Note that a robust and accurate clustering model will have a lower value of withiness and a higher value of betweenness. However, these values depend on the number of clusters that is K, which is chosen before building the model. Now, based on this, we will train the K-means model for different K values that are a number of predefined clusters. We will start **K = 2** to 10, as follows:

```
wcss_list = []
for i in range(2, 10):
    centers, cluster_assignments, wcss = kmeans(x_train, len(x_
train[0]), i)
    wcss_list.append(wcss)
```

Now, let's discuss how we can take the advantage of the Elbow method for determining the number of clusters. We calculated the cost function WCSS as a function of a number of clusters for the K-means algorithm applied to home data based on all the features, as follows:

```
plt.figure(figsize=(12, 24))
plt.subplot(211)
plt.plot(range(2, 10), wcss_list)
plt.xlabel('No of Clusters')
plt.ylabel('WCSS')
plt.title("WCSS vs Clusters")
>>>
```

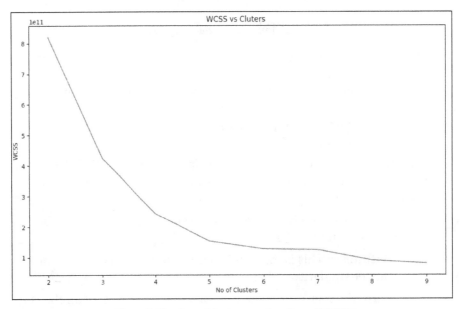

Figure 7: Number of clusters as a function of WCSS

We will try to reuse this lesson in upcoming examples using K-means too. Now, it can be observed that a big drop occurs when **k = 5**. Therefore, we chose the number of clusters to be **5** as discussed in figure 7. Basically, this is the one after the last big drop. This means that the optimal number of cluster for our dataset that we need to set before we start training the K-means model is **5**.

6. Clustering analysis.

From figure 8, it is clear that most houses fall in **cluster 3 (4655 houses)** and then in **cluster 4 (3356 houses)**. The x-axis shows the price and the y-axis shows the lot size for each house. We can also observe that the **cluster 1** has only a few houses and potentially in longer distances, but it is also expensive. So, it is most likely that you will not find a nearer neighborhood to interact with if you buy a house that falls in this cluster. However, if you like more human interaction and budget is a constraint, you should probably try buying a house from cluster 2, 3, 4, or 5:

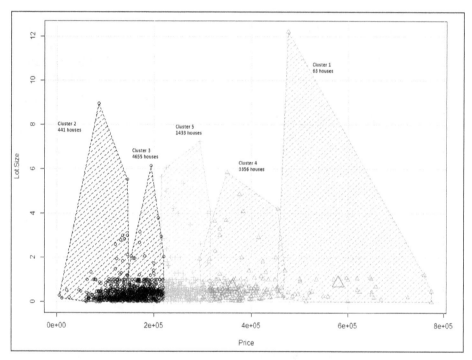

Figure 8: Clusters of neighborhoods, that is,. homogeneous houses fall in same clusters

To make the analysis, we dumped the output in RStudio and generated the clusters shown in figure 6. The R script can be found on my GitHub repositories at `https://github.com/rezacsedu/ScalaAndSparkForBigDataAnalytics`. Alternatively, you can write your own script and do the visualization accordingly.

Predictive Models for Clustering Audio Files

For clustering music with audio data, the data points are the feature vectors from the audio files. If two points are close together, it means that their audio features are similar. We want to discover which audio files belong to the same neighborhood because these clusters will probably be a good way to organize your music files:

1. Loading audio files with TensorFlow and Python.

   Some common input types in ML algorithms are audio and image files. This shouldn't come as a surprise because sound recordings and photographs are raw, redundant, ab nd often noisy representations of semantic concepts. ML is a tool to help handle these complications. These data files have various implementations, for example, an audio file can be an MP3 or WAV.

   Reading files from a disk isn't exactly a ML-specific ability. You can use a variety of Python libraries to load files onto the memory, such as Numpy or Scipy. Some developers like to treat the data preprocessing step separately from the ML step. However, I believe that this is also a part of the whole analytics process.

   Since this is a TensorFlow book, I will try to use something from the TensorFlow built-in operator to list files in a directory called `tf.train.match_filenames_once()`. We can then pass this information along to a `tf.train.string_input_producer()` queue operator. This way, we can access a filename one at a time, without loading everything at once. Here's the structure of this method:

   ```
   match_filenames_once(pattern,name=None)
   ```

   This method takes two parameters: `pattern` and `name`. `pattern` signifies a file pattern or 1D tensor of file patterns. The `name` is used to signify the name of the operations. However, this parameter is optional. Once invoked, this method saves the list of matching patterns, so as the name implies, it is only computed once.

   Finally, a variable that is initialized to the list of files matching the pattern(s) is returned by this method. Once we have finished reading the metadata and the audio files, we can decode the file to retrieve usable data from the given filename. Now, let's get started. First, we need to import necessary packages and Python modules, as follows:

   ```python
   import tensorflow as tf
   import numpy as np
   from bregman.suite import *
   from tensorflow.python.framework import ops
   ```

```
import warnings
import random
```

Now we can start reading the audio files from the directory specified. First, we need to store filenames that match a pattern containing a particular file extension, for example, `.mp3`, `.wav`, and so on. Then, we need to set up a pipeline for retrieving filenames randomly. Now, the code natively reads a file in TensorFlow. Then, we run the reader to extract the file data. Use can use following code for this task:

```
filenames = tf.train.match_filenames_once('./audio_dataset/*.wav')
count_num_files = tf.size(filenames)
filename_queue = tf.train.string_input_producer(filenames)
reader = tf.WholeFileReader()
filename, file_contents = reader.read(filename_queue)
chromo = tf.placeholder(tf.float32)
max_freqs = tf.argmax(chromo, 0)
```

Well, once we have read the data and metadata about all the audio files, the next and immediate tasks are to capture the audio features that will be used by K-means for the clustering purpose.

2. Extracting features and preparing feature vectors.

ML algorithms are typically designed to use feature vectors as input; however, sound files are a very different format. We need a way to extract features from sound files to create feature vectors.

It helps to understand how these files are represented. If you've ever seen a vinyl record, you've probably noticed the representation of audio as grooves indented in the disk. Our ears interpret audio from a series of vibrations through the air. By recording the vibration properties, our algorithm can store sound in a data format. The real world is continuous but computers store data in discrete values.

The sound is digitalized into a discrete representation through an **Analog to Digital Converter (ADC)**. You can think about sound as a fluctuation of a wave over time. However, this data is too noisy and difficult to comprehend. An equivalent way to represent a wave is by examining the frequencies that make it up at each time interval. This perspective is called the frequency domain.

It's easy to convert between time domain and frequency domain using a mathematical operation called a discrete Fourier transform (commonly known as the Fast Fourier transform). We will use this technique to extract a feature vector out of our sound.

A sound may produce 12 kinds of pitch. In music terminology, the 12 pitches are C, C#, D, D#, E, F, F#, G, G#, A, A#, and B. Figure 9 shows how to retrieve the contribution of each pitch in a 0.1-second interval, resulting in a matrix with 12 rows. The number of columns grows as the length of the audio file increases. Specifically, there will be **10*t** columns for a **t** second audio.

This matrix is also called a chromogram of the audio. But first, we need to have a placeholder for TensorFlow to hold the chromogram of the audio and the maximum frequency:

```
chromo = tf.placeholder(tf.float32)
max_freqs = tf.argmax(chromo, 0)
```

The next task that we can perform is that we can write a method that can extract these chromograms for the audio files. It can look as follows:

```
def get_next_chromogram(sess):
    audio_file = sess.run(filename)
    F = Chromagram(audio_file, nfft=16384, wfft=8192, nhop=2205)
    return F.X, audio_file
```

The workflow of the previous code is as follows:

- ° First, pass in the filename and use these parameters to describe 12 pitches every 0.1 seconds.

- ° Finally, represent the values of a 12-dimensional vector 10 times a second.

The chromogram output that we extract using the previous method will be a matrix, as visualized in figure 10. A sound clip can be read as a chromogram, and a chromogram is a recipe for generating a sound clip. Now, we have a way to convert audio and matrices. As you have learned, most ML algorithms accept feature vectors as a valid form of data. That being said, the first ML algorithm we'll look at is K-means clustering:

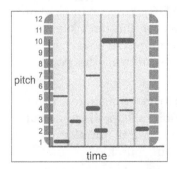

Figure 9: The visualization of the chromogram matrix where the x-axis represents time and the y-axis represents pitch class. The green markings indicate a presence of that pitch at that time

To run the ML algorithms on our chromogram, we first need to decide how we're going to represent a feature vector. One idea is to simplify the audio by only looking at the most significant pitch class per time interval, as shown in figure 10:

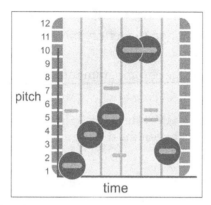

Figure 10: The most influential pitch at every time interval is highlighted. You can think of it as the loudest pitch at each time interval

Now, we will count the number of times each pitch shows up in the audio file. Figure 11 shows this data as a histogram, forming a 12-dimensional vector. If we normalize the vector so that all the counts add up to **1**, then we can easily compare audio of different lengths:

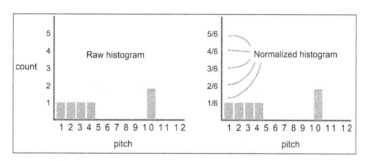

Figure 11: We count the frequency of the loudest pitches heard at each interval to generate this histogram, which acts as our feature vector

Now that we have the chromagram, we need to use it to extract the audio feature to construct a feature vector. You can use the following method for this:

```
def extract_feature_vector(sess, chromo_data):
    num_features, num_samples = np.shape(chromo_data)
    freq_vals = sess.run(max_freqs, feed_dict={chromo: chromo_
data})
```

```
    hist, bins = np.histogram(freq_vals, bins=range(num_features +
))
    normalized_hist = hist.astype(float) / num_samples
    return normalized_hist
```

The workflow of the previous code is as follows:

- ° Create an operation to identify the pitch with the biggest contribution.

- ° Now, convert the chromogram into a feature vector.

- ° After this, we will construct a matrix where each row is a data item.

- ° Now, if you can hear the audio clip, you can imagine and differentiate between the different audio files. However, this is just intuition.

Therefore, we cannot rely on this, but we should inspect them visually. So, we will invoke the previous method to extract the feature vector from each audio file and plot the feature. The whole operation should look as follows:

```
def get_dataset(sess):
    num_files = sess.run(count_num_files)
    coord = tf.train.Coordinator()
    threads = tf.train.start_queue_runners(coord=coord)
    xs = list()
    names = list()
    plt.figure()
    for _ in range(num_files):
        chromo_data, filename = get_next_chromogram(sess)
        plt.subplot(1, 2, 1)
        plt.imshow(chromo_data, cmap='Greys',
interpolation='nearest')
        plt.title('Visualization of Sound Spectrum')
        plt.subplot(1, 2, 2)
        freq_vals = sess.run(max_freqs, feed_dict={chromo: chromo_
data})
        plt.hist(freq_vals)
        plt.title('Histogram of Notes')
        plt.xlabel('Musical Note')
        plt.ylabel('Count')
        plt.savefig('{}.png'.format(filename))
        plt.clf()
        plt.clf()
        names.append(filename)
```

```
    x = extract_feature_vector(sess, chromo_data)
    xs.append(x)
xs = np.asmatrix(xs)
return xs, names
```

The previous code should plot the audio features of each audio file in the histogram as follows:

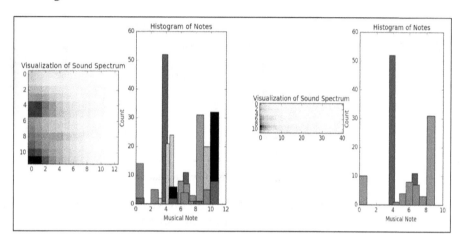

Figure 12: The ride audio files show a similar histogram

You can see some examples of audio files that we are trying to cluster based on their audio features. As you can see, the two on the right appear to have similar histograms. The two on the left also have similar sound spectrums:

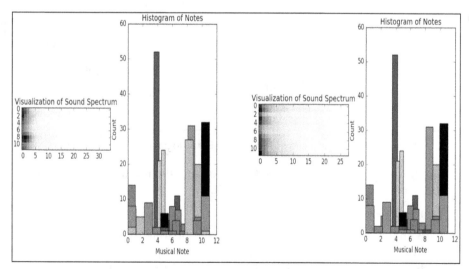

Figure 13: The crash cymbal audio files show a similar histogram

Now, the target is to develop K-means so that it is able to group these sounds together accurately. We will look at the high-level view of the cough audio files, as shown in the following figure:

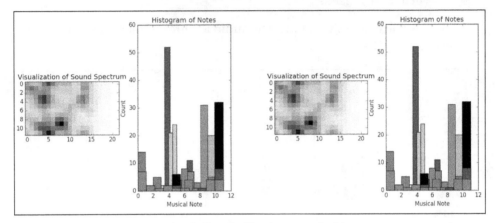

Figure 14: The cough audio files show a similar histogram

Finally, we have the scream audio files that have a similar histogram and audio spectrum, but of course are different compared to others:

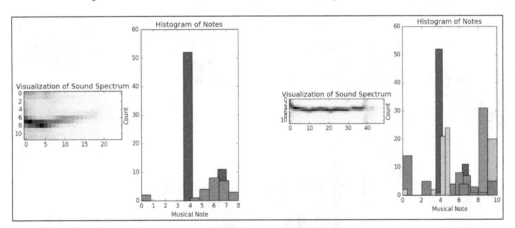

Figure 15: The scream audio files show a similar histogram and audio spectrum

Now, we can imagine our problem. We have the features ready for training the K-means model. Let's start doing it.

1. Training K-means model.

    Now that the feature vector is ready, it's time to feed this to the K-means model for clustering the feature presented in figure 10. The idea is that the midpoint of all the points in a cluster is called a centroid.

Depending on the audio features we choose to extract, a centroid can capture concepts such as loud sound, high-pitched sound, or saxophone-like sound. Therefore, it's important to note that the K-means algorithm assigns non-descript labels, such as cluster 1, cluster 2, or cluster 3. First, we can write a method that computes the initial cluster centroids as follows:

```
def initial_cluster_centroids(X, k):
    return X[0:k, :]
```

Now, the next task is to randomly assign the cluster number to each data point based on the initial cluster assignment. This time we can use another method:

```
def assign_cluster(X, centroids):
    expanded_vectors = tf.expand_dims(X, 0)
    expanded_centroids = tf.expand_dims(centroids, 1)
    distances = tf.reduce_sum(tf.square(tf.subtract(expanded_
vectors, expanded_centroids)), 2)
    calc_wss = tf.reduce_sum(tf.reduce_min(distances, 0))
    mins = tf.argmin(distances, 0)
    return mins, calc_wss
```

The previous method computes the minimum distance and WCSS for the clustering evaluation in the later steps. Then, we need to update the centroid to check and make sure if there are any changes that occur in the cluster assignment:

```
def recompute_centroids(X, Y):
    sums = tf.unsorted_segment_sum(X, Y, k)
    counts = tf.unsorted_segment_sum(tf.ones_like(X), Y, k)
    return sums / counts
```

Now that we have defined many variables, it's time to initialize them using `local_variable_initializer()`, as follows:

```
init_op = tf.local_variables_initializer()
```

Finally, we can perform the training. Forthis, the `audioClusterin()` method takes the number of tentative clusters k and iterates the training up to the maximum iteration, as follows:

```
def audioClustering(k, max_iterations ):
    with tf.Session() as sess:
        sess.run(init_op)
        X, names = get_dataset(sess)
        centroids = initial_cluster_centroids(X, k)
        i, converged = 0, False
        while not converged and i < max_iterations:
            i += 1.
```

```
        Y, wcss_updated = assign_cluster(X, centroids)
        centroids = sess.run(recompute_centroids(X, Y))
    wcss = wcss_updated.eval()
    print(zip(sess.run(Y)), names)
return wcss
```

The previous method returns the cluster cost, WCSS, and also prints the cluster number against each audio file. So, we have been able to finish the training step. Now, the next task is to evaluate the K-means clustering quality.

2. Evaluating the model.

Here, we will evaluate the clustering quality from two perspectives. First, we will observe the predicted cluster number. Secondly, we will also try to find the optimal value of k as a function of WCSS. So, we will iterate the training for **K = 2** to say **10** and observe the clustering result. However, first, let's create two empty lists to hold the values of k and WCSS in each step:

```
wcss_list = []
k_list = []
```

Now, let's iterate the training using the for loop as follows:

```
for k in range(2, 9):
    random.seed(12345)
    wcss = audioClustering(k, 100)
    wcss_list.append(wcss)
    k_list.append(k)
```

This prints the following output:

```
([(0,), (1,), (1,), (0,), (1,), (0,), (0,), (0,), (0,), (0,),
(0,)],
['./audio_dataset/scream_1.wav', './audio_dataset/Crash-Cymbal-3.
wav', './audio_dataset/Ride_Cymbal_1.wav', './audio_dataset/Ride_
Cymbal_2.wav', './audio_dataset/Crash-Cymbal-2.wav', './audio_
dataset/Ride_Cymbal_3.wav', './audio_dataset/scream_3.wav', './
audio_dataset/scream_2.wav', './audio_dataset/cough_2.wav', './
audio_
dataset/cough_1.wav', './audio_dataset/Crash-Cymbal-1.wav'])

([(0,), (1,), (2,), (2,), (2,), (2,), (2,), (1,), (2,), (2,),
(2,)],
['./audio_dataset/Ride_Cymbal_2.wav', './audio_dataset/Crash-
Cymbal-3.wav', './audio_dataset/cough_1.wav', './audio_dataset/
Crash-
Cymbal-2.wav', './audio_dataset/scream_2.wav', './audio_dataset/
Ride_Cymbal_3.wav', './audio_dataset/Crash-Cymbal-1.wav', './
```

```
udio_
dataset/Ride_Cymbal_1.wav', './audio_dataset/cough_2.wav', './
audio_
dataset/scream_1.wav', './audio_dataset/scream_3.wav'])

([(0,), (1,), (2,), (3,), (2,), (2,), (2,), (2,), (2,), (2,),
(2,)],
['./audio_dataset/Ride_Cymbal_2.wav', './audio_dataset/Ride_
Cymbal_3.
wav', './audio_dataset/cough_1.wav', './audio_dataset/Crash-
Cymbal-1.
wav', './audio_dataset/scream_3.wav', './audio_dataset/cough_2.
wav',
'./audio_dataset/Crash-Cymbal-2.wav', './audio_dataset/Ride_
Cymbal_1.
wav', './audio_dataset/Crash-Cymbal-3.wav', './audio_dataset/
scream_1.wav', './audio_dataset/scream_2.wav'])

([(0,), (1,), (2,), (3,), (4,), (0,), (0,), (4,), (0,), (0,),
(0,)],
['./audio_dataset/cough_1.wav', './audio_dataset/scream_1.wav',
'./
audio_dataset/Crash-Cymbal-1.wav', './audio_dataset/Ride_Cymbal_2.
wav', './audio_dataset/Crash-Cymbal-3.wav', './audio_dataset/
scream_2.wav', './audio_dataset/cough_2.wav', './audio_dataset/
Ride_Cymbal_1.wav', './audio_dataset/Crash-Cymbal-2.wav', './
audio_
dataset/Ride_Cymbal_3.wav', './audio_dataset/scream_3.wav'])

([(0,), (1,), (2,), (3,), (4,), (5,), (2,), (2,), (2,), (4,),
(2,)],
['./audio_dataset/scream_3.wav', './audio_dataset/Ride_Cymbal_2.
wav',
'./audio_dataset/cough_1.wav', './audio_dataset/Crash-Cymbal-2.
wav',
'./audio_dataset/Crash-Cymbal-3.wav', './audio_dataset/scream_2.
wav',
'./audio_dataset/Crash-Cymbal-1.wav', './audio_dataset/cough_2.
wav',
'./audio_dataset/Ride_Cymbal_3.wav', './audio_dataset/Ride_
Cymbal_1.
wav', './audio_dataset/scream_1.wav'])

([(0,), (1,), (2,), (3,), (4,), (5,), (6,), (5,), (6,), (5,),
(5,)],
['./audio_dataset/cough_2.wav', './audio_dataset/Ride_Cymbal_3.
```

```
av',
'./audio_dataset/scream_1.wav', './audio_dataset/Ride_Cymbal_2.
wav',
'./audio_dataset/Crash-Cymbal-1.wav', './audio_dataset/cough_1.
wav',
'./audio_dataset/scream_2.wav', './audio_dataset/Crash-Cymbal-3.
wav',
'./audio_dataset/scream_3.wav', './audio_dataset/Ride_Cymbal_1.
wav',
'./audio_dataset/Crash-Cymbal-2.wav'])

([(0,), (1,), (2,), (3,), (4,), (5,), (6,), (7,), (6,), (6,),
(1,)],
['./audio_dataset/Crash-Cymbal-1.wav', './audio_dataset/scream_3.
wav', './audio_dataset/Ride_Cymbal_3.wav', './audio_dataset/
Crash-Cymbal-3.wav', './audio_dataset/Crash-Cymbal-2.wav', './
audio_dataset/cough_2.wav', './audio_dataset/cough_1.wav', './
audio_
dataset/Ride_Cymbal_1.wav', './audio_dataset/Ride_Cymbal_2.wav',
'./
audio_dataset/scream_1.wav', './audio_dataset/scream_2.wav'])

([(0,), (1,), (2,), (3,), (4,), (5,), (6,), (7,), (8,), (1,),
(7,)],
['./audio_dataset/scream_2.wav', './audio_dataset/Ride_Cymbal_1.
wav',
'./audio_dataset/Crash-Cymbal-2.wav', './audio_dataset/Ride_
Cymbal_3.
wav', './audio_dataset/Ride_Cymbal_2.wav', './audio_dataset/
scream_3.
wav', './audio_dataset/Crash-Cymbal-1.wav', './audio_dataset/
cough_1.
wav', './audio_dataset/cough_2.wav', './audio_dataset/Crash-
Cymbal-3.
wav', './audio_dataset/scream_1.wav'])
```

These values signify that each audio file is clustered and the cluster number has been assigned (the first bracket is the cluster number, the contents in the second bracket is the filename). However, it is difficult to judge the accuracy from this output. One naïve approach would be to compare each file with figure 12 to figure 15. Alternatively, let's adopt a better approach that we used in the first example that is the elbow method. For this, I have created a dictionary using two lists that are `k_list` and `wcss_list` computed previously, as follows:

```
dict_list = zip(k_list, wcss_list)
```

```
my_dict = dict(dict_list)
print(my_dict)
```

The previous code produces the following output:

```
{2: 2.8408628007260428, 3: 2.3755930780867365, 4:
0.9031724736903582,
5: 0.7849431270192495, 6: 0.872767581979385, 7:
0.62019339653673422,
8: 0.70075249251166494, 9: 0.86645706880532057}
```

From the previous output, you can see a sharp drop in WCSS for **k = 4**, and this is generated in the third iteration. So, based on this minimum evaluation, we can take a decision about the following clustering assignment:

```
Ride_Cymbal_1.wav => 2
Ride_Cymbal_2.wav => 0
cough_1.wav => 2
cough_2.wav =>2
Crash-Cymbal-1.wav =>3
Crash-Cymbal-2.wav => 2
scream_1.wav => 2
scream_2.wav => 2
```

Now that we have seen two complete examples of using K-means, there is another example called kNN. This is typically a supervised ML algorithm. In the next section, we will see how we can train this algorithm in an unsupervised way for a regression task.

Using kNN for Predictive Analytics

kNN is non-parametric and instance-based and is used in supervised learning. It is a robust and versatile classifier, frequently used as a benchmark for complex classifiers such as **Neural Networks (NNs)** and **Support Vector Machines (SVMs)**. kNN is commonly used in economic forecasting, data compression, and genetics based on their expression profiling.

Working Principles of kNN

The idea of kNN is that from a set of features **x** we try to predict the labels **y**. Thus, kNN falls in a supervised learning family of algorithms. Informally, this means that we are given a labeled dataset consisting of training observations (x, y). Now, the task is to model the relationship between x and y so that the function $f: X \rightarrow Y$ learns from the unseen observation x. The function $f(x)$ can confidently predict the corresponding label y prediction on a point z by looking at a set of nearest neighbors.

However, the actual method of prediction depends on whether or not we are doing regression (continuous) or classification (discrete). For discrete classification targets, the prediction may be given by a maximum voting scheme weighted by the distance to the prediction point:

$$f(z) = \max_j \sum_{i=1}^{k} \varphi(d_{ij}) l_{ij}$$

Here, our prediction, *f(z)*, is the maximum weighted value of all classes, *j*, where the weighted distance from the prediction point to the training point, *i*, is given by φ *(dij)*, where *d* indicates the distance between two points. On the other hand, *Iij* is just an indicator function if point *i* is in class *j*.

For continuous regression targets, the prediction is given by a weighted average of all *k* points nearest to the prediction:

$$f(z) = \frac{1}{k} \sum_{i=1}^{k} \varphi(d_i)$$

From the previous two equations, it is clear that the prediction is heavily dependent on the choice of the distance metric, *d*. There are many different specifications of distance metrics such as L1 and L2 metrics can be used for the textual distances:

A straightforward way to weigh the distances is by the distance itself. Points that are further away from our prediction should have less impact than the nearer points. The most common way to weigh is the normalized inverse of the distance. We will implement this method in the next section.

Implementing a kNN-Based Predictive Model

To illustrate how making predictions with the nearest neighbors works in TensorFlow, we will use the 1970s Boston housing dataset, which is available through the UCI ML repository at `https://archive.ics.uci.edu/ml/machine-learning-databases/housing/housing.data`. The following table shows the basic description of the dataset:

Header	Significance
CRIM	Per capita crime rate by town
N	Proportion of the residential land zones
INDUS	Proportion of non-retail business acres
CHAS	Charles river dummy variable
NOX	Nitric oxide concentration/10 M
RM	Average # of rooms per building
AGE	Proportion of buildings built prior to 1940
DIS	Weighted distances to employment centers
RAD	Index of radian highway access
TAX	Full tax rate value per $10k
PTRATIO	Pupil/teacher ratio by town
B	1,000*(Bk-0.63)^2, Bk=prop. of blocks
LSTAT	% lower status of pop
MEDV	Median value of homes in $1,000s

Here, we will predict the median neighborhood housing value that is the last value named MEDV as a function of several features. Since we consider the training set the trained model, we will find kNNs to the prediction points and do a weighted average of the target value. Let's get started:

1. Loading required libraries and packages.

   As an entry point, we import necessary libraries and packages that will be needed to do predictive analytics using kNN with TensorFlow:

   ```
   import matplotlib.pyplot as plt
   import numpy as np
   import random
   import os
   import tensorflow as tf
   import requests
   from tensorflow.python.framework import ops
   import warnings
   ```

2. Resetting the default graph and disabling the TensorFlow warning.

   We need to reset the default TensorFlow graph using the `reset_default_graph()` function from TensorFlow. You must also disable all warnings due to the absence of GPU on your device:

   ```
   warnings.filterwarnings("ignore")
   os.environ['TF_CPP_MIN_LOG_LEVEL'] = '3'
   ops.reset_default_graph()
   ```

3. Loading and preprocessing the dataset.

    First, we will load and parse the dataset using the `get()` function from the requests package as follows:

    ```
    housing_url = 'https://archive.ics.uci.edu/ml/machine-learning-
    databases/housing/housing.data'
    housing_header = ['CRIM', 'ZN', 'INDUS', 'CHAS', 'NOX', 'RM',
    'AGE', 'DIS', 'RAD', 'TAX', 'PTRATIO', 'B', 'LSTAT', 'MEDV']
    num_features = len(housing_header)
    housing_file = requests.get(housing_url)
    housing_data = [[float(x) for x in y.split(' ') if len(x)>=1] for
    y in housing_file.text.split('\n') if len(y)>=1]
    ```

     For more information on how the previous code works, please see the documentation of requests package at `http://docs.python-requests.org/en/master/user/quickstart/`.

    Then, we will separate features (predictor) from the labels:

    ```
    y_vals = np.transpose([np.array([y[len(housing_header)-1] for y in
    housing_data])])
    x_vals = np.array([[x for i,x in enumerate(y) if housing_header[i]
    in housing_header] for y in housing_data])
    ```

    Now, to get some idea of the features and labels, let's print them as follows:

    ```
    print(y_vals)
    >>>
    [[ 24. ]
     [ 21.6]
     [ 34.7]
     [ 33.4]
     [ 36.2]
     [ 28.7]
     [ 22.9]
     [ 27.1]
     [ 16.5]
     [ 18.9]
     [ 15. ]
     ...]
    ```

So, the labels are okay to work with, and these are also continuous values. Now, let's see the features:

```
print(x_vals)
>>>
[[  6.32000000e-03    1.80000000e+01    2.31000000e+00 ...,
3.96900000e+02
      4.98000000e+00    2.40000000e+01]
 [  2.73100000e-02    0.00000000e+00    7.07000000e+00 ...,
3.96900000e+02
      9.14000000e+00    2.16000000e+01]
 [  2.72900000e-02    0.00000000e+00    7.07000000e+00 ...,
3.92830000e+02
      4.03000000e+00    3.47000000e+01]
 ...,
 [  6.07600000e-02    0.00000000e+00    1.19300000e+01 ...,
3.96900000e+02
      5.64000000e+00    2.39000000e+01]
 [  1.09590000e-01    0.00000000e+00    1.19300000e+01 ...,
3.93450000e+02

      6.48000000e+00    2.20000000e+01]
 [  4.74100000e-02    0.00000000e+00    1.19300000e+01 ...,
3.96900000e+02
      7.88000000e+00    1.19000000e+01]]
```

Well, if you see these values, they are pretty unscaled to be fed to a predictive model. Thus, we need to apply the min-max scaling to get a better structure of the features so that an estimator scales and translates each feature individually, and it ensures that it is in the given range on the training set, that is, between zero and one. Since features are most important in predictive analytics, we should take special care of them. The following line of code does the min-max scaling:

```
x_vals = (x_vals - x_vals.min(0)) / x_vals.ptp(0)
```

Now let's print them again to check to make sure what's changed:

```
print(x_vals)
>>>
[[  0.00000000e+00    1.80000000e-01    6.78152493e-02 ...,
1.00000000e+008.96799117e-02    4.22222222e-01]
 [  2.35922539e-04    0.00000000e+00    2.42302053e-01 ...,
1.00000000e+002.04470199e-01    3.68888889e-01]
 [  2.35697744e-04    0.00000000e+00    2.42302053e-01 ...,
9.89737254e-016.34657837e-02    6.60000000e-01] ...,
 [  6.11892474e-04    0.00000000e+00    4.20454545e-01 ...,
1.00000000e+001.07891832e-01    4.20000000e-01]
```

```
  [ 1.16072990e-03   0.00000000e+00   4.20454545e-01 ...,
9.91300620e-01
    1.31070640e-01   3.77777778e-01]
  [ 4.61841693e-04   0.00000000e+00   4.20454545e-01 ...,
1.00000000e+00
    1.69701987e-01   1.53333333e-01]]
```

1. Preparing the training and test set.

    Since our features are already scaled, now it's time to split the data into train and test sets. Now, we split the x and y values into the train and test sets. We will create the training set by selecting about 75% of the rows at random and leave the remaining 25% for the test set:

    ```
    train_indices = np.random.choice(len(x_vals), int(len(x_
    vals)*0.75), replace=False)
    test_indices = np.array(list(set(range(len(x_vals))) - set(train_
    indices)))
    x_vals_train = x_vals[train_indices]
    x_vals_test = x_vals[test_indices]
    y_vals_train = y_vals[train_indices]
    y_vals_test = y_vals[test_indices]
    ```

2. Preparing the placeholders for the tensors.

    First, we will declare the batch size. Ideally, the batch size should be equal to the size of features in the test set:

    ```
    batch_size=len(x_vals_test)
    ```

    Then, we need to declare the placeholders for the TensorFlow tensors, as follows:

    ```
    x_data_train = tf.placeholder(shape=[None, num_features],
    dtype=tf.float32)
    x_data_test = tf.placeholder(shape=[None, num_features], dtype=tf.
    float32)
    y_target_train = tf.placeholder(shape=[None, 1], dtype=tf.float32)
    y_target_test = tf.placeholder(shape=[None, 1], dtype=tf.float32)
    ```

3. Defining the distance metrics.

    For this example, we are going to use the L1 distance. The reason is that using L2 did not give a better result in my case:

    ```
    distance = tf.reduce_sum(tf.abs(tf.subtract(x_data_train,
    tf.expand_dims(x_data_test,1))), axis=2)
    ```

4. Implementing kNN.

Now, it's time to implement kNN. This will predict the nearest neighbors by getting the minimum distance index. The `kNN()` method does the trick. There are several steps for doing this, as follows:

1. Get the minimum distance index.

2. Compute the prediction function. To do this, we will use the `top_k()`, function, which returns the values and indices of the largest values in a tensor. Since we want the indices of the smallest distances, we will instead find the k-biggest negative distances. Since we are predicting continuous values that is regression task, we also declare the predictions and **Mean Squared Error (MSE)** of the target values.

3. Calculate the number of loops over training data.

4. Initialize the global variables.

5. Iterate the training over the number of loops calculated in step 3.

Now, here's the function of kNN. It takes the number of initial neighbors and starts the computation. Note that although it is a widely used convention, here I will make it a variable to do some tuning, as shown in the following code:

```
def kNN(k):
    topK_X, topK_indices = tf.nn.top_k(tf.negative(distance), k=k)
    x_sums = tf.expand_dims(tf.reduce_sum(topK_X, 1), 1)
    x_sums_repeated = tf.matmul(x_sums,tf.ones([1, k],
tf.float32))
    x_val_weights = tf.expand_dims(tf.div(topK_X, x_sums_
repeated), 1)
    topK_Y = tf.gather(y_target_train, topK_indices)
    prediction = tf.squeeze(tf.matmul(x_val_weights,topK_Y),
axis=[1])
  mse = tf.div(tf.reduce_sum(tf.square(tf.subtract(prediction, y_
target_test))), batch_size)
    num_loops = int(np.ceil(len(x_vals_test)/batch_size))
    init_op = tf.global_variables_initializer()
    with tf.Session() as sess:
        sess.run(init_op)
        for i in range(num_loops):
            min_index = i*batch_size
            max_index = min((i+1)*batch_size,len(x_vals_
train))
            x_batch = x_vals_test[min_index:max_index]
            y_batch = y_vals_test[min_index:max_index]
            predictions = sess.run(prediction, feed_dict={x_
```

```
data_train: x_vals_train, x_data_test: x_batch, y_target_train: y_
vals_train, y_target_test: y_batch})
                batch_mse = sess.run(mse, feed_dict={x_data_train:
x_vals_train, x_data_test: x_batch, y_target_train: y_vals_train,
y_target_test: y_batch})
    return batch_mse
```

5. Evaluating the classification/regression.

    Note that this function does not return the optimal mse value, that is, the lowest mse value, but varies over different k values, so this is a hyperparameter to be tuned. One potential technique would be to iterate the method for $k = 2$ to, say, 11 and keeping track of the optimal k value that forces kNN() to produce the lowest mse value. First, we define a method that iterates several times from 2 to 11 and returns two separate lists for mse and k respectively:

```
mse_list = []
k_list = []
def getOptimalMSE_K():
    mse = 0.0
    for k in range(2, 11):
        mse = kNN(k)
        mse_list.append(mse)
        k_list.append(k)
    return k_list, mse_list
```

Now, it's time to invoke the previous method and find the optimal k value for which the kNN produces the lowest mse value. Upon receiving the two lists, we create a dictionary and use the min() method to return the optimal k value, as follows:

```
k_list, mse_list  = getOptimalMSE_K()
dict_list = zip(k_list, mse_list)
my_dict = dict(dict_list)
print(my_dict)
optimal_k = min(my_dict, key=my_dict.get)
>>>
{2: 7.6624126, 3: 10.184645, 4: 8.9112329, 5: 11.29573, 6:
13.341181, 7: 14.406253, 8: 13.923589, 9: 14.915736, 10:
13.920851}
```

Now, let's print the `Optimal k value` for which we get the lowest `mse` value:

```
print("Optimal K value: ", optimal_k)
mse = min(mse_list)
print("Minimum mean square error: ", mse)
>>>
Optimal K value: 2 minimum mean square error: 7.66241
```

6. Running the best kNN.

   Now we have the optimal k, so we will entertain calculating the nearest neighbor. This time we will try to return the matrices for the predicted and actual labels:

```
def bestKNN(k):
    topK_X, topK_indices = tf.nn.top_k(tf.negative(distance), k=k)
    x_sums = tf.expand_dims(tf.reduce_sum(topK_X, 1), 1)
    x_sums_repeated = tf.matmul(x_sums,tf.ones([1, k],
tf.float32))
    x_val_weights = tf.expand_dims(tf.div(topK_X, x_sums_
repeated), 1)
    topK_Y = tf.gather(y_target_train, topK_indices)
    prediction = tf.squeeze(tf.matmul(x_val_weights,topK_Y),
axis=[1])
    num_loops = int(np.ceil(len(x_vals_test)/batch_size))
    init_op = tf.global_variables_initializer()
    with tf.Session() as sess:
        sess.run(init_op)
        for i in range(num_loops):
            min_index = i*batch_size
            max_index = min((i+1)*batch_size,len(x_vals_
train))

            x_batch = x_vals_test[min_index:max_index]
            y_batch = y_vals_test[min_index:max_index]
```

predictions = sess.run(prediction, feed_dict={x_data_train: x_vals_train, x_data_test: x_batch, y_target_train: y_vals_train, y_target_test: y_batch})

```
    return predictions, y_batch
```

7. Evaluating the best kNN.

   Now, we will invoke the `bestKNN()` method with the optimal value of k that was calculated in the previous step, as follows:

```
predicted_labels, actual_labels = bestKNN(optimal_k)
```

Now, I would like to measure the prediction accuracy. Are you wondering why? I know the reason. You're right. There is no significant reason for calculating the accuracy or precision since we are predicting the continuous values that is labels. Even so, I would like to show you whether it works or not:

```
def getAccuracy(testSet, predictions):
 correct = 0
 for x in range(len(testSet)):
     if(np.round(testSet[x]) == np.round(predictions[x])):
             correct += 1
 return (correct/float(len(testSet))) * 100.0
accuracy = getAccuracy(actual_labels, predicted_labels)
print('Accuracy: ' + repr(accuracy) + '%')
>>>
Accuracy: 17.322834645669293%
```

The previous `getAccuracy()` method computes the accuracy, which is quite low. This is obvious and there is no exertion. This also implies that the previous method is pointless. However, if you are about to predict discrete values, this method will obviously help you. Try it yourself with suitable data and combinations of the previous code.

But do not to be disappointed; we have another way of looking at how our predictive model performs. We can still plot a histogram showing the predicted versus actual labels that are a prediction and actual distribution:

```
bins = np.linspace(5, 50, 45)
plt.hist(predicted_labels, bins, alpha=1.0, facecolor='red',
label='Prediction')
plt.hist(actual_labels, bins, alpha=1.0, facecolor='green',
label='Actual')
plt.title('predicted vs actual values')
plt.xlabel('Median house price in $1,000s')
plt.ylabel('count')
plt.legend(loc='upper right')
plt.show()
>>>
```

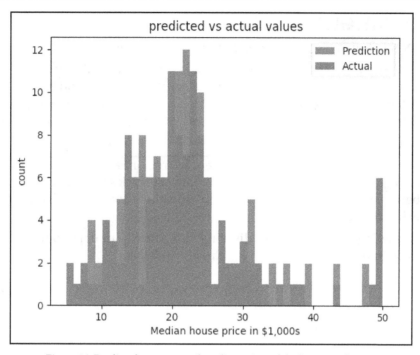

Figure 16: Predicted versus actual median prices of the houses in $1,000s

Summary

In this lesson, we have discussed unsupervised learning from a theoretical and practical perspective. We have seen how we can make use of predictive analytics and find out how we can take advantage of it to cluster records belonging to a certain group or class for a dataset of unsupervised observations. We have discussed unsupervised learning and clustering using K-means. In addition, we have seen how we can fine tune the clustering using the Elbow method for better predictive accuracy. We have also seen how to predict neighborhoods using K-means, and then, we have seen another example of clustering audio clips based on their audio features. Finally, we have seen how we can use unsupervised kNN for predicting the nearest neighbors.

In the next lesson, we will discuss the wonderful field of text analytics using TensorFlow. Text analytics is a wide area in **natural language processing (NLP)**, and ML is useful in many use cases, such as sentiment analysis, chatbots, email spam detection, text mining, and natural language processing. You will learn how to use TensorFlow for text analytics with a focus on use cases of text classification from the unstructured spam prediction and movie review dataset. Based on the spam filtering dataset, we will develop predictive models using a LR algorithm with TensorFlow

Assessments

1. kNN falls in a _____ learning family of algorithms.

2. State whether the following statement is True or False: A cluster is a collection of objects that have a similarity between them and are dissimilar to the objects belonging to other clusters. If a collection of objects is provided, clustering algorithms put these objects into groups based on similarity.

3. What is the main objective of unsupervised learning?

4. State whether the following statement is True or False: In a clustering task, an algorithm groups related features into categories by analyzing similarities between input examples, where similar features are clustered and marked using circles.

5. Clustering analysis is about dividing data samples or data points and putting them into corresponding _____ classes or clusters.

   1. Heterogynous
   2. Linear
   3. Homogeneous
   4. Similar.

4
Using Reinforcement Learning for Predictive Analytics

As a human being, we learn from past experiences. We haven't become so charming by accident. Years of positive compliments as well as negative criticism have all helped shape us into who we are today. We learn how to ride a bike by trying out different muscle movements until it just clicks. When you perform actions, you're sometimes rewarded immediately. This is all about **reinforcement learning (RL)**.

This lesson is all about designing a machine learning system driven by criticisms and rewards. We will see how to apply reinforcement learning algorithms for the predictive model on real-life datasets.

In a nutshell, the following topics will be covered throughout this lesson:

- Reinforcement learning
- Reinforcement learning for predictive analytics
- Notation, policy, and utility in RL
- Developing a multiarmed bandit's predictive model
- Developing a stock price predictive model

Reinforcement Learning

From a technical perspective, whereas supervised and unsupervised learning appears at opposite ends of the spectrum, RL exists somewhere in the middle. It's not supervised learning because the training data comes from the algorithm deciding between exploration and exploitation. And it's not unsupervised because the algorithm receives feedback from the environment. As long as you are in a situation where performing an action in a state produces a reward, you can use reinforcement learning to discover a good sequence of actions to take the maximum expected rewards.

The goal of an RL agent will be to maximize the total reward that it receives in the long run. The third main sub element is the `value` function.

While the rewards determine an immediate desirability of the states, the values indicate the long-term desirability of states, taking into account the states that may follow and the available rewards in these states. The `value` function is specified with respect to the chosen policy. During the learning phase, an agent tries actions that determine the states with the highest value, because these actions will get the best amount of reward in the long run.

Reinforcement Learning in Predictive Analytics

Figure 1 shows a person making decisions to arrive at their destination. Moreover, suppose on your drive from home to work you always choose the same route. But one day your curiosity takes over and you decide to try a different path in hopes for a shorter commute. This dilemma of trying out new routes or sticking to the best-known route is an example of exploration versus exploitation:

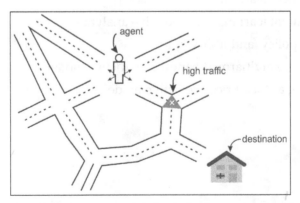

Figure 1: An agent always try to reach the destination passing through route

Reinforcement learning techniques are being used in many areas. A general idea that is being pursued right now is creating an algorithm that doesn't need anything apart from a description of its task. When this kind of performance is achieved, it will be applied virtually everywhere.

Notation, Policy, and Utility in RL

You may notice that reinforcement learning jargon involves anthropomorphizing the algorithm into taking actions in situations to receive rewards. In fact, the algorithm is often referred to as an agent that acts with the environment. You can just think of it like an intelligent hardware agent sensing with sensors and interacting with the environment using its actuators.

Therefore, it shouldn't be a surprise that much of RL theory is applied in robotics. Figure 2 demonstrates the interplay between states, actions, and rewards. If you start at state **s1**, you can perform action **a1** to obtain a reward r (**s1, a1**). Actions are represented by arrows, and states are represented by circles:

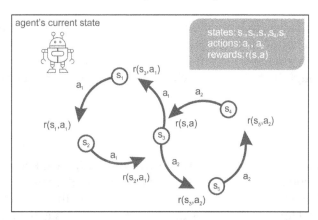

Figure 2: An agent is performing an action on a state produces a reward

A robot performs actions to change between different states. But how does it decide which action to take? Well, it's all about using different or a concrete policy.

Policy

In reinforcement learning lingo, we call the strategy a policy. The goal of reinforcement learning is to discover a good strategy. One of the most common ways to solve it is by observing the long-term consequences of actions in each state. The short-term consequence is easy to calculate: that's just the reward. Although performing an action yields an immediate reward, it's not always a good idea to greedily choose the action with the best reward.

That's a lesson in life too because the most immediate best thing to do might not always be the most satisfying in the long run. The best possible policy is called the optimal policy, and it's often the holy grail of RL as shown in figure 3, which shows the optimal action given any state:

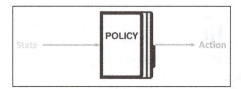

Figure 3: A policy defines an action to be taken in a given state

We've so far seen one type of policy where the agent always chooses the action with the greatest immediate reward, called a greedy policy. Another simple example of a policy is arbitrarily choosing an action, called random policy. If you come up with a policy to solve a reinforcement learning problem, it's often a good idea to double-check that your learned policy performs better than both the random and greedy policies.

In addition, we will also see how to develop another robust policy called policy gradients, where a neural network learns a policy for picking actions by adjusting its weights through gradient descent using feedback from the environment. We will see that although both the approaches are used, policy gradient is more direct and optimistic.

Utility

The long-term reward is called a utility. It turns out that, if we know the utility of performing an action at a state, then it's easy to solve reinforcement learning. For example, to decide which action to take, we simply select the action that produces the highest utility. However, uncovering these utility values is the harder part to be sorted out. The utility of performing an action a at a state **s** is written as a function $Q(s, a)$, called the utility function that predicts the expected immediate reward plus rewards following an optimal policy gave the state-action input which is shown in figure 4:

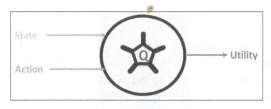

Figure 4: Using a utility function

Most reinforcement learning algorithms boil down to just three main steps: infer, do, and learn. During the first step, the algorithm selects the best action (*a*) given a state (*s*) using the knowledge it has so far. Next, it does the action to find out the reward (*r*) as well as the next state (*s'*). Then it improves its understanding of the world using the newly acquired knowledge *(s, r, a, s')*. However, this is just a naive way to calculate the utility; you would agree on this too.

Now, the question is what could be a more robust way to compute it? Here are two cents from my side. We can calculate the utility of a particular state-action pair *(s, a)* by recursively considering the utilities of future actions. The utility of your current action is influenced not just by the immediate reward, but also the next best action, as shown in the following formula:

$$Q(s,a) = r(s,a) + \gamma \max Q(s',a')$$

In the previous formula, *s'* denotes the next state, and *a'* denotes the next action. The reward of taking action *a* in state *s* is denoted by *r(s, a)*. Here, γ is a hyperparameter that you get to choose, called the discount factor. If γ is *0*, then the agent chooses the action that maximizes the immediate reward. Higher values of γ will make the agent put more importance in considering long-term consequences.

In practice, we have more hyperparameters to be considered. For example, if a vacuum cleaner robot is expected to learn to solve tasks quickly but not necessarily optimally, we might want to set a faster learning rate. Alternatively, if a robot is allowed more time to explore and exploit, we might tune down the learning rate. Let's call the learning rate α, and change our utility function as follows (note that when *a = 1*, both the equations are identical):

$$Q(s,a) \rightarrow Q(s,a) + \alpha\left(r(s,a) + \gamma \max Q(s',a') - Q(s,a)\right)$$

In summary, an RL problem can be solved if we know this *Q(s, a)* function. Here comes the machine learning strategy called neural networks, which are a way to approximate functions given enough training data. Also, TensorFlow is the perfect tool to deal with neural networks because it comes with many essential algorithms.

In the next two sections, we will see two examples of such implementation with TensorFlow. The first example is a naïve way of developing a multiarmed bandit agent for the predictive model. Then, the second example is a bit more advanced using neural network implementation for stock price prediction.

Developing a Multiarmed Bandit's Predictive Model

One of the simplest RL problems is called n-armed bandits. The thing is there are n-many slot machines but each has different fixed payout probability. The goal is to maximize the profit by always choosing the machine with the best payout.

As mentioned earlier, we will also see how to use policy gradient that produces explicit outputs. For our multiarmed bandits, we don't need to formalize these outputs on any particular state. To be simpler, we can design our network such that it will consist of just a set of weights that are corresponding to each of the possible arms to be pulled in the bandit. Then, we will represent how good an agent thinks to pull each arm to make maximum profit. A naive way is to initialize these weights to 1 so that the agent will be optimistic about each arm's potential reward.

To update the network, we can try choosing an arm with a greedy policy that we discussed earlier. Our policy is such that the agent receives a reward of either 1 or -1 once it has issued an action. I know this is not a realistic imagination but most of the time the agent will choose an action randomly that corresponds to the largest expected value.

We will start developing a simple but effective bandit agent incrementally for solving multiarmed bandit problems. At first, there will be no state, that is, we will have a stateless agent. Then, we will see that using a stateless bandit agent to solve a complex problem is so biased that we cannot use it in real life.

Then we will increase the agent complexity by adding or converting the sample bandits into contextual bandits. The contextual bandits then will be a state full agent so can solve our predicting problem more efficiently. Finally, we will further increase the agent complexity by converting the textual bandits to full RL agent before deploying it:

1. Load the required library.

   Load the required library and packages/modules needed:

   ```
   import tensorflow as tf
   import tensorflow.contrib.slim as slim
   import numpy as np
   ```

2. Defining bandits.

    For this example, I am using a four-armed bandit. The `getBandit` function that generates a random number from a normal distribution has the mean of 0. The lower the Bandit number, the more likely a positive reward will be awarded. As stated earlier, this is just a naïve but greedy way to train the agent so that it learns to choose a bandit that will generate not only the positive but also the maximum reward. Here I have listed the bandits so that Bandit 4 most often provides a positive reward:

    ```
    def getBandit(bandit):
        ''
        This function creates the reward to the bandits on the basis
    of randomly generated numbers. It then returns either a positive
    or negative reward.
        ''
        random_number = np.random.randn(1)
        if random_number > bandit:
            return 1
        else:
            return -1
    ```

3. Developing an agent for the bandits.

    The following code creates a very simple neural agent consisting of a set of values for each of the `bandits`. Each value is estimated to be 1 based on the return value from the `bandits`. We use a policy gradient method to update the agent by moving the value for the selected action toward the received reward. At first, we need to reset the graph as follows:

    ```
    tf.reset_default_graph()
    ```

    Then, the next two lines do the actual choosing by establishing the feed-forward part of the network:

    ```
    weight_op = tf.Variable(tf.ones([num_bandits]))
    action_op = tf.argmax(weight_op,0)
    ```

    Now, before starting the training process, we need to initiate the training process itself. Since we already know the reward, now it's time to feed them and choose an action in the network to compute the loss and use it to update the network:

    ```
    reward_holder = tf.placeholder(shape=[1],dtype=tf.float32)
    action_holder = tf.placeholder(shape=[1],dtype=tf.int32)
    responsible_weight = tf.slice(weight_op,action_holder,[1])
    ```

We need to define the objective function that is loss:

```
loss = -(tf.log(responsible_weight)*reward_holder)
```

And then let's make the training process slow to make it exhaustive utilizing the learning rate:

```
LR = 0.001
```

We then use the gradient descent `optimizer` and instantiate the `training` operation:

```
optimizer = tf.train.GradientDescentOptimizer(learning_rate=LR)
training_op = optimizer.minimize(loss)
```

Now, it's time to define the training parameters such as a total number of iterations to train the agent, `reward` function, and a `random` action. The reward here sets the scoreboard for `bandits` to `0`, and by choosing a random action, we set the probability of taking a random action:

```
total_episodes = 10000
total_reward = np.zeros(num_bandits)
chance_of_random_action = 0.1
```

Finally, we initialize the global variables:

```
init_op = tf.global_variables_initializer()
```

4. Training the agent.

   We need to train the agent by taking actions to the environment and receiving rewards. We start by creating a TensorFlow session and launch the TensorFlow graph. Then, iterate the training process up to a total number of iterations. Then, we choose either a random act or one from the network. We then compute the reward from picking one of the `bandits`. Then, we make the training process consistent and update the network. Finally, we update the scoreboard:

```
with tf.Session() as sess:
    sess.run(init_op)
    i = 0
    while i < total_episodes:
        if np.random.rand(1) < chance_of_random_action:
            action = np.random.randint(num_bandits)
        else:
            action = sess.run(action_op)
                reward = getBandit(bandits[action])
            _,resp,ww = sess.run([training_op,responsible_
weight,weight_op], feed_dict={reward_holder:[reward],action_
holder:[action]})
```

```
        total_reward[action] += reward
        if i % 50 == 0:
            print("Running reward for all the " + str(num_bandits)
+ " bandits: " + str(total_reward))
        i+=1
```

Now let's evaluate the above model as follows:

```
print("The agent thinks bandit " + str(np.argmax(ww)+1) + " would
be the most efficient one.")
if np.argmax(ww) == np.argmax(-np.array(bandits)):
    print(" and it was right at the end!")
else:
    print(" and it was wrong at the end!")
>>>
```

The first iteration generates the following output:

```
Running reward for all the 4 bandits: [-1. 0. 0. 0.]
Running reward for all the 4 bandits: [ -1. -2. 14. 0.]
...
Running reward for all the 4 bandits: [ -15. -7. 340. 21.]
Running reward for all the 4 bandits: [ -15. -10. 364. 22.]
The agent thinks Bandit 3 would be the most efficient one and it
was wrong at the end!
```

The second iteration generates a different result as follows:

```
Running reward for all the 4 bandits: [ 1. 0. 0. 0.]
Running reward for all the 4 bandits: [ -1. 11. -3. 0.]
Running reward for all the 4 bandits: [ -2. 1. -2. 20.]
...
Running reward for all the 4 bandits: [ -7. -2. 8. 762.]
Running reward for all the 4 bandits: [ -8. -3. 8. 806.]
The agent thinks Bandit 4 would be the most efficient one and it
was right at the end!
```

Now that if you see the limitation of this agent being a stateless agent so randomly predicts which bandits to choose. In that situation, there are no environmental states, and the agent must simply learn to choose which action is best to take. To get rid of this problem, we can think of developing contextual bandits.

Using the contextual bandits, we can introduce and make the proper utilization of the state. The state consists of an explanation of the environment that the agent can use to make more intelligent and informed actions. The thing is that instead of using a single bandit we can chain multiple bandits together. So what would be the function of the state? Well, the state of the environment tells the agent to choose a bandit from the available list. On the other hand, the goal of the agent is to learn the best action for any number of bandits.

This way, the agent faces an issue since each bandit may have different reward probabilities for each arm and agent needs to learn how to perform an action on the state of the environment. Otherwise, the agent cannot achieve the maximum reward possible:

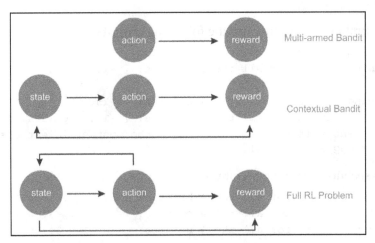

Figure 5: Stateless versus contextual bandits

As mentioned earlier, to get rid of this issue, we can build a single-layer neural network so that it can take a state and yield an action. Now, similar to the random bandits, we can use a policy-gradient update method too so that the network update is easier to take actions for maximizing the reward. This simplified way of posting an RL problem is referred to as the contextual bandit.

5. Developing contextual bandits.

This example was adopted and extended based on "Simple Reinforcement Learning with TensorFlow Part 1.5: Contextual Bandits" By Arthur Juliani published at https://medium.com/.

At first, let's define our contextual bandits. For this example, we will see how to use three four-armed bandits, that is, each Bandit has four arms that can be pulled to make an action. Since each bandit is contextual and has a state, so their arms have different success probabilities. This requires different actions to be performed to yield the best predictive result.

Here, we define a class named `contextual_bandit()` consisting of a constructor and two user defined functions: `getBandit()` and `pullArm()`. The `getBandit()` function generates a random number from a normal distribution with a mean of 0. The lower the Bandit number, the more likely a positive reward will be returned to be utilized. We want our agent to learn to choose the banditarm that will most often give a positive reward. Of course, it depends on the bandit presented. This constructor lists out all of our bandits. We assume the current state being armed 4, 2, 3, and 1 that is the most optimal respectively.

Also, if you see carefully, most of the reinforcement learning algorithms follow similar implementation patterns. Thus, it's a good idea to create a class with the relevant methods to reference later, such as an abstract class or interface:

```python
class contextualBandit():
    def __init__(self):
        self.state = 0
        self.bandits = np.array([[0.2,0,-0.0,-5], [0.1,-5,1,0.25],
[0.3,0.4,-5,0.5], [-5,5,5,5]])
        self.num_bandits = self.bandits.shape[0]
        self.num_actions = self.bandits.shape[1]
        def getBandit(self):
        '''
        This function returns a random state for each episode.
        '''
        self.state = np.random.randint(0, len(self.bandits))
        return self.state
        def pullArm(self,action):
        '''
        This function creates the reward to the bandits on the
basis of randomly generated numbers. It then returns either a
positive or negative reward that is action
        '''
        bandit = self.bandits[self.state, action]
        result = np.random.randn(1)
        if result > bandit:
            return 1
        else:
            return -1
```

6. Developing a policy-based agent.

The following class `ContextualAgent` helps develop our simple, but very effective neural and contextual agent. We supply the current state as input and it then returns an action that is conditioned on the state of the environment. This is the most important step toward making a stateless agent a stateful one to be able to solve a full RL problem.

Here, I tried to develop this agent such that it uses a single set of weights for choosing a particular arm given a bandit. The policy gradient method is used to update the agent by moving the value for a particular action toward achieving maximum reward:

```
class ContextualAgent():
    def __init__(self, lr, s_size,a_size):
        '''
        This function establishes the feed-forward part of the
network. The agent takes a state and produces an action -that is.
contextual agent
        '''
        self.state_in= tf.placeholder(shape=[1], dtype=tf.int32)
        state_in_OH = slim.one_hot_encoding(self.state_in, s_size)
        output = slim.fully_connected(state_in_OH, a_size,biases_
initializer=None, activation_fn=tf.nn.sigmoid, weights_
initializer=tf.ones_initializer())
        self.output = tf.reshape(output, [-1])
        self.chosen_action = tf.argmax(self.output,0)
        self.reward_holder = tf.placeholder(shape=[1], dtype=tf.
float32)
        self.action_holder = tf.placeholder(shape=[1], dtype=tf.
int32)
        self.responsible_weight = tf.slice(self.output, self.
action_holder,[1])
        self.loss = -(tf.log(self.responsible_weight)*self.reward_
holder)
        optimizer = tf.train.GradientDescentOptimizer(learning_
rate=lr)
        self.update = optimizer.minimize(self.loss)
```

7. Training the contextual bandit agent.

At first, we clear the default TensorFlow graph:

```
tf.reset_default_graph()
```

Then, we define some parameters that will be used to train the agent:

```
lrarning_rate = 0.001 # learning rate
chance_of_random_action = 0.1 # Chance of a random action.
max_iteration = 10000 #Max iteration to train the agent.
```

Now, before starting the training, we need to load the bandits and then our agent:

```
contextualBandit = contextualBandit() #Load the bandits.
contextualAgent = ContextualAgent(lr=lrarning_rate, s_
size=contextualBandit.num_bandits, a_size=contextualBandit.num_
actions) #Load the agent.
```

Now, to maximize the objective function toward total rewards, `weights` is used to evaluate to look into the network. We also set the scoreboard for `bandits` to `0` initially:

```
weights = tf.trainable_variables()[0]
total_reward = np.zeros([contextualBandit.num_
bandits,contextualBandit.num_actions])
```

Then, we initialize all the variables using `global_variables_initializer()` function:

```
init_op = tf.global_variables_initializer()
```

Finally, we will start the training. The training is similar to the random one we have done in the preceding example. However, here the main objective of the training is to compute the mean reward for each of the bandits so that we can evaluate the agent's prediction accuracy later on by utilizing them:

```
with tf.Session() as sess:
    sess.run(init_op)
    i = 0
    while i < max_iteration:
        s = contextualBandit.getBandit() #Get a state from the
environment.
        #Choose a random action or one from our network.
        if np.random.rand(1) < chance_of_random_action:
            action = np.random.randint(contextualBandit.num_
actions)
        else:
            action = sess.run(contextualAgent.chosen_action,feed_
dict={contextualAgent.state_in:[s]})
        reward = contextualBandit.pullArm(action) #Get our reward
for taking an action given a bandit.
        #Update the network.
        feed_dict={contextualAgent.reward_
holder:[reward],contextualAgent.action_
```

```
holder:[action],contextualAgent.state_in:[s]}
        _,ww = sess.run([contextualAgent.update,weights], feed_
dict=feed_dict)
        #Update our running tally of scores.
        total_reward[s,action] += reward
        if i % 500 == 0:
            print("Mean reward for each of the " +
str(contextualBandit.num_bandits) + " bandits: " + str(np.
mean(total_reward,axis=1)))
        i+=1
>>>
Mean reward for each of the 4 bandits: [ 0. 0. -0.25 0. ]
Mean reward for each of the 4 bandits: [ 25.75 28.25 25.5 28.75]
...
Mean reward for each of the 4 bandits: [ 488.25 489. 473.5 440.5 ]
Mean reward for each of the 4 bandits: [ 518.75 520. 499.25
465.25]
Mean reward for each of the 4 bandits: [ 546.5 547.75 525.25
490.75]
```

8. Evaluating the agent.

   Now, that we have the mean reward for all the four bandits, it's time to utilize them to predict something interesting, that is, which bandit's arm will maximize the reward. Well, at first we can initialize some variables to estimate the prediction accuracy as well:

```
right_flag = 0
wrong_flag = 0
```

Then let's start evaluating the agent's prediction performance:

```
for a in range(contextualBandit.num_bandits):
    print("The agent thinks action " + str(np.argmax(ww[a])+1) + "
for bandit " + str(a+1) + " would be the most efficient one.")
    if np.argmax(ww[a]) == np.argmin(contextualBandit.bandits[a]):
        right_flag += 1
        print(" and it was right at the end!")
    else:
        print(" and it was wrong at the end!")
        wrong_flag += 1
>>>
The agent thinks action 4 for Bandit 1 would be the most efficient
one and it was right at the end!
The agent thinks action 2 for Bandit 2 would be the most efficient
one and it was right at the end!
The agent thinks action 3 for Bandit 3 would be the most efficient
```

```
ne and it was right at the end!
The agent thinks action 1 for Bandit 4 would be the most efficient
one and it was right at the end!
```

As you can see, all the predictions made are right predictions. Now we can compute the accuracy as follows:

```
prediction_accuracy = (right_flag/right_flag+wrong_flag)
print("Prediction accuracy (%):", prediction_accuracy * 100)
>>>
Prediction accuracy (%): 100.0
```

Fantastic, well done! We have managed to design and develop a more robust bandit agent by means of a contextual agent that can accurately predict which arm, that is, the action of a bandit that would help to achieve the maximum reward, that is, profit.

In the next section, we will see another interesting but very useful application for stock price prediction, where we will see how to develop a policy-based Q Learning agent out of the box of the RL.

Developing a Stock Price Predictive Model

An emerging area for applying is the stock market trading, where a trader acts like a reinforcement agent since buying and selling (that is, action) particular stock changes the state of the trader by generating profit or loss, that is, reward. The following figure shows some of the most active stocks on July 15, 2017 (for an example):

Stocks: Most Actives >

Symbol	Last Price	Change	% Change
BAC Bank of America Corporation	24.21	-0.41	-1.67%
AMD Advanced Micro Devices, Inc.	13.92	0.39	2.88%
JNS Janus Capital Group, Inc.	14.17	-0.08	-0.56%
S Sprint Corporation	8.55	0.35	4.27%
F Ford Motor Company	11.68	0.08	0.69%

Figure 6: https://finance.yahoo.com/

Now, we want to develop an intelligent agent that will predict stock prices such that a trader will buy at a low price and sell at a high price. However, this type of prediction is not so easy and is dependent on several parameters such as the current number of stocks, recent historical prices, and most importantly, on the available budget to be invested for buying and selling.

The states in this situation are a vector containing information about the current budget, current number of stocks, and a recent history of stock prices (the last 200 stock prices). So each state is a 202-dimensional vector. For simplicity, there are only three actions to be performed by a stock market agent: buy, sell, and hold.

So, we have the state and action, what else do you need? Policy, right? Yes, we should have a good policy, so based on that an action will be performed in a state. A simple policy can consist of the following rules:

- Buying (that is, action) a stock at the current stock price (that is, state) decreases the budget while incrementing the current stock count

- Selling a stock trades it in for money at the current share price

- Holding does neither, and performing this action simply waits for a particular time period and yields no reward

To find the stock prices, we can use the `yahoo_finance` library in Python. A general warning you might experience is "**HTTPError: HTTP Error 400: Bad Request**". But keep trying.

Now, let's try to get familiar with this module:

```
>>> from yahoo_finance import Share
>>> msoft = Share('MSFT')
>>> print(msoft.get_open())
72.24=
>>> print(msoft.get_price())
72.78
>>> print(msoft.get_trade_datetime())
2017-07-14 20:00:00 UTC+0000
>>>
```

So as of July 14, 2017, the stock price of Microsoft Inc. went higher, from 72.24 to 72.78, which means about a 7.5% increase. However, this small and just one-day data doesn't give us any significant information. But, at least we got to know the present state for this particular stock or instrument.

To install `yahoo_finance`, issue the following command:

```
$ sudo pip3 install yahoo_finance
```

Now it would be worth looking at the historical data. The following function helps us get the historical data for Microsoft Inc:

```
def get_prices(share_symbol, start_date, end_date, cache_filename):
    try:
        stock_prices = np.load(cache_filename)
    except IOError:
        share = Share(share_symbol)
        stock_hist = share.get_historical(start_date, end_date)
        stock_prices = [stock_price['Open'] for stock_price in stock_
hist]
        np.save(cache_filename, stock_prices)
    return stock_prices
```

The `get_prices()` method takes several parameters such as the share symbol of an instrument in the stock market, the opening date, and the end date. You will also like to specify and cache the historical data to avoid repeated downloading. Once you have downloaded the data, it's time to plot the data to get some insights.

The following function helps us to plot the price:

```
def plot_prices(prices):
    plt.title('Opening stock prices')
    plt.xlabel('day')
    plt.ylabel('price ($)')
    plt.plot(prices)
    plt.savefig('prices.png')
```

Now we can call these two functions by specifying a real argument as follows:

```
if __name__ == '__main__':
    prices = get_prices('MSFT', '2000-07-01', '2017-07-01',
'historical_stock_prices.npy')
    plot_prices(prices)
```

Here I have chosen a wide range for the historical data of 17 years to get a better insight. Now, let's take a look at the output of this data:

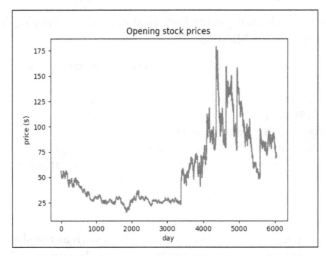

Figure 7: Historical stock price data of Microsoft Inc. from 2000 to 2017

The goal is to learn a policy that gains the maximum net worth from trading in the stock market. So what will a trading agent be achieving in the end? Figure 8 gives you some clue:

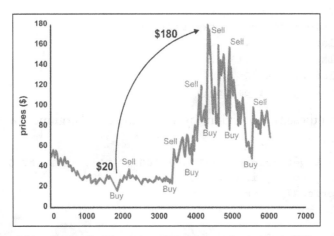

Figure 8: Some insight and a clue that shows, based on the current price, up to $160 profit can be made

Well, figure 8 shows that if the agent buys a certain instrument with price $20 and sells at a peak price say at $180, it will be able to make $160 reward, that is, profit.

So, implementing such an intelligent agent using RL algorithms is a cool idea?

From the previous example, we have seen that for a successful RL agent, we need two operations well defined, which are as follows:

- How to select an action
- How to improve the utility Q-function

To be more specific, given a state, the decision policy will calculate the next action to take. On the other hand, improve Q-function from a new experience of taking an action.

Also, most reinforcement learning algorithms boil down to just three main steps: infer, perform, and learn. During the first step, the algorithm selects the best action (a) given a state (s) using the knowledge it has so far. Next, it performs the action to find out the reward (r) as well as the next state (s').

Then, it improves its understanding of the world using the newly acquired knowledge *(s, r, a, s')* as shown in the following figure:

$$\text{Infer}(s) \Rightarrow a$$
$$\text{Do}(s,a) \Rightarrow r, s'$$
$$\text{Learn}(s, r, a, s')$$

Figure 9: Steps to be performed for implementing an intelligent stock price prediction agent

Now, let's start implementing the decision policy based on which action will be taken for buying, selling, or holding a stock item. Again, we will do it an incremental way. At first, we will create a random decision policy and evaluate the agent's performance.

But before that, let's create an abstract class so that we can implement it accordingly:

```
class DecisionPolicy:
    def select_action(self, current_state, step):
        pass
    def update_q(self, state, action, reward, next_state):
        pass
```

The next task that can be performed is to inherit from this superclass to implement a random decision policy:

```
class RandomDecisionPolicy(DecisionPolicy):
    def __init__(self, actions):
        self.actions = actions
    def select_action(self, current_state, step):
        action = self.actions[random.randint(0, len(self.actions) -
1)]
        return action
```

The previous class did nothing except defining a function named `select_action`
`()`, which will randomly pick an action without even looking at the state.

Now, if you would like to use this policy, you can run it on the real-world stock price data. This function takes care of exploration and exploitation at each interval of time, as shown in the following figure that form states S1, S2, and S3. The policy suggests an action to be taken, which we may either choose to exploit or otherwise randomly explore another action. As we get rewards for performing an action, we can update the policy function over time:

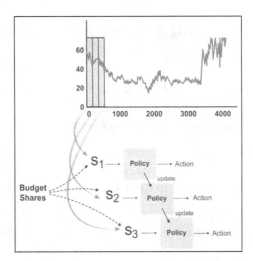

Figure 10: A rolling window of some size iterates through the stock prices over time

Fantastic, so we have the policy and now it's time to utilize this policy to make decisions and return the performance. Now, imagine a real scenario—suppose you're trading on Forex or ForTrade platform, then you can recall that you also need to compute the portfolio and the current profit or loss, that is, reward. Typically, these can be calculated as follows:

```
portfolio = budget + number of stocks * share value
reward = new_portfolio - current_portfolio
```

At first, we can initialize values that depend on computing the net worth of a portfolio, where the state is a `hist+2`dimensional vector. In our case, it would be 202 dimensional. Then we define the range of tuning the range up to:

Length of the prices selected by the user query – (history + 1), since we start from 0, we subtract 1 instead. Then, we should calculate the updated value of the portfolio and from the portfolio, we can calculate the value of the reward, that is, profit.

Also, we have already defined our random policy, so we can then select an action from the current policy. Then, we repeatedly update the portfolio values based on the action in each iteration and the new portfolio value after taking the action can be calculated. Then, we need to compute the reward from taking an action at a state. Nevertheless, we also need to update the policy after experiencing a new action. Finally, we compute the final portfolio worth:

```python
def run_simulation(policy, initial_budget, initial_num_stocks, prices,
hist, debug=False):
    budget = initial_budget
    num_stocks = initial_num_stocks
    share_value = 0
    transitions = list()
    for i in range(len(prices) - hist - 1):
        if i % 100 == 0:
            print('progress {:.2f}%'.format(float(100*i) /
(len(prices) - hist - 1)))
        current_state = np.asmatrix(np.hstack((prices[i:i+hist],
budget, num_stocks)))
        current_portfolio = budget + num_stocks * share_value
        action = policy.select_action(current_state, i)
        share_value = float(prices[i + hist + 1])
        if action == 'Buy' and budget >= share_value:
            budget -= share_value
            num_stocks += 1
        elif action == 'Sell' and num_stocks > 0:
            budget += share_value
            num_stocks -= 1
        else:
            action = 'Hold'
        new_portfolio = budget + num_stocks * share_value
        reward = new_portfolio - current_portfolio
        next_state = np.asmatrix(np.hstack((prices[i+1:i+hist+1],
budget, num_stocks)))
        transitions.append((current_state, action, reward, next_
state))
        policy.update_q(current_state, action, reward, next_state)
```

```
    portfolio = budget + num_stocks * share_value
    if debug:
        print('${}\t{} shares'.format(budget, num_stocks))
    return portfolio
```

The previous simulation predicts a somewhat good result; however, it produces random results too often. Thus, to obtain a more robust measurement of success, let's run the simulation a couple of times and average the results. Doing so may take a while to complete, say 100 times, but the results will be more reliable:

```
def run_simulations(policy, budget, num_stocks, prices, hist):
    num_tries = 100
    final_portfolios = list()
    for i in range(num_tries):
        final_portfolio = run_simulation(policy, budget, num_stocks,
prices, hist)
        final_portfolios.append(final_portfolio)
    avg, std = np.mean(final_portfolios), np.std(final_portfolios)
    return avg, std
```

The previous function computes the average portfolio and the standard deviation by iterating the previous simulation function 100 times. Now, it's time to evaluate the previous agent. As already stated, there will be three possible actions to be taken by the stock trading agent such as buy, sell, and hold. We have a state vector of 202 dimension and budget only $1000. Then, the evaluation goes as follows:

```
actions = ['Buy', 'Sell', 'Hold']
    hist = 200
    policy = RandomDecisionPolicy(actions)
    budget = 1000.0
    num_stocks = 0
    avg, std=run_simulations(policy,budget,num_stocks,prices, hist)
    print(avg, std)
>>>
1512.87102405 682.427384814
```

The first one is the mean and the second one is the standard deviation of the final portfolio. So, our stock prediction agent predicts that as a trader you/we could make a profit about $513. Not bad. However, the problem is that since we have utilized a random decision policy, the result is not so reliable. To be more specific, the second execution will definitely produce a different result:

```
>>>
1518.12039077 603.15350649
```

Therefore, we should develop a more robust decision policy. Here comes the use of neural network-based QLearning for decision policy. Next, we will see a new hyperparameter epsilon to keep the solution from getting stuck when applying the same action over and over. The lesser its value, the more often it will randomly explore new actions:

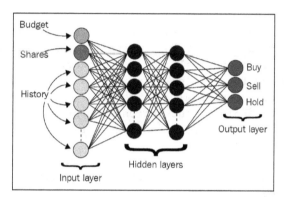

Figure 11: The input is the state space vector with three outputs, one for each output's Q-value

Next, I am going to write a class containing their functions:

- `Constructor`: This helps to set the hyperparameters from the Q-function. It also helps to set the number of hidden nodes in the neural networks. Once we have these two, it helps to define the input and output tensors. It then defines the structure of the neural network. Further, it defines the operations to compute the utility. Then, it uses an optimizer to update model parameters to minimize the loss and sets up the session and initializes variables.

- `select_action`: This function exploits the best option with probability 1-epsilon.

- `update_q`: This updates the Q-function by updating its model parameters.

Refer to the following code:

```
class QLearningDecisionPolicy(DecisionPolicy):
    def __init__(self, actions, input_dim):
        self.epsilon = 0.9
        self.gamma = 0.001
        self.actions = actions
        output_dim = len(actions)
        h1_dim = 200
        self.x = tf.placeholder(tf.float32, [None, input_dim])
        self.y = tf.placeholder(tf.float32, [output_dim])
        W1 = tf.Variable(tf.random_normal([input_dim, h1_dim]))
        b1 = tf.Variable(tf.constant(0.1, shape=[h1_dim]))
```

```
        h1 = tf.nn.relu(tf.matmul(self.x, W1) + b1)
        W2 = tf.Variable(tf.random_normal([h1_dim, output_dim]))
        b2 = tf.Variable(tf.constant(0.1, shape=[output_dim]))
        self.q = tf.nn.relu(tf.matmul(h1, W2) + b2)
        loss = tf.square(self.y - self.q)
        self.train_op = tf.train.GradientDescentOptimizer(0.01).
minimize(loss)
        self.sess = tf.Session()
        self.sess.run(tf.initialize_all_variables())
    def select_action(self, current_state, step):
        threshold = min(self.epsilon, step / 1000.)
        if random.random() < threshold:
            # Exploit best option with probability epsilon
            action_q_vals = self.sess.run(self.q, feed_
dict={self.x: current_state})
            action_idx = np.argmax(action_q_vals)
            action = self.actions[action_idx]
        else:
            # Random option with probability 1 - epsilon
            action = self.actions[random.randint(0, len(self.
actions) - 1)]
        return action
    def update_q(self, state, action, reward, next_state):
        action_q_vals = self.sess.run(self.q, feed_dict={self.x:
state})
        next_action_q_vals = self.sess.run(self.q, feed_
dict={self.x: next_state})
        next_action_idx = np.argmax(next_action_q_vals)
        action_q_vals[0, next_action_idx] = reward + self.gamma *
next_action_q_vals[0, next_action_idx]
        action_q_vals = np.squeeze(np.asarray(action_q_vals))
        self.sess.run(self.train_op, feed_dict={self.x: state, self.y:
action_q_vals})
```

Summary

In this lesson, we have discussed a wonderful field of machine learning called reinforcement learning with TensorFlow. We have discussed it from the theoretical as well as practical point of view. Reinforcement learning is the natural tool when a problem can be framed by states that change due to actions that can be taken by an agent to discover rewards. There are three primary steps in implementing the algorithm: infer the best action from the current state, perform the action, and learn from the results.

We have seen how to implement RL agents for making predictions by knowing the `action`, `state`, `policy`, and `utility` functions. We have seen how to develop RL-based agents using random policy as well as neural network-based QLearning policy. QLearning is an approach to solve reinforcement learning, where you develop an algorithm to approximate the utility function (Q-function). Once a good enough approximation is found, you can start inferring best actions to take from each state. In particular, we have seen two step-by-step examples that show how we could develop a multiarmed bandit agent and a stock price prediction agent with very good accuracy. But, be advised that the actual stock market is a much more complicated beast, and the techniques used in this lesson generalize too many situations.

This is more or less the end of our little journey with TensorFlow. I hope you'd a smooth journey and gained a lot of knowledge on TensorFlow.

I wish you all the best for your future projects. Keep learning and exploring!

Assessments

1. In reinforcement learning lingo, we call the _____ a policy.

2. State whether the following statement is True or False: The goal of reinforcement learning is to discover a good strategy. One of the most common ways to solve it is by observing the long-term consequences of actions in each state.

3. We need to train the agent by taking actions to the environment and receiving _____.

4. State whether the following statement is True or False: Using the contextual bandits, we cannot introduce and make the proper utilization of the state.

5. To find the stock prices, we can use the _____ library in Python.

   1. get_prices
   2. plot_prices
   3. yahoo_finance
   4. finance_yahoo

Assessment Answers

Lesson 1: From Data to Decisions – Getting Started with TensorFlow

Question Number	Answer
1	2
2	True
3	True
4	<ul><li>A set of `tf.Operation` objects: This is used to represent units of computation to be performed</li><li>A `tf.Tensor` object: This is used to represent units of data that control the dataflow between operations</li></ul>
5	3

Lesson 2: Putting Data in Place – Supervised Learning for Predictive Analytics

Question Number	Answer
1	supervised learning, unsupervised learning, and reinforcement learning
2	False
3	`model_params = {"learning_rate": LEARNING_RATE}"`
4	True
5	4

Lesson 3: Clustering Your Data – Unsupervised Learning for Predictive Analytics

Question Number	Answer
1	Supervised
2	True
3	The main objective of the unsupervised learning algorithms is to explore the unknown/hidden patterns in the input data that are unlabeled
4	True
5	3

Lesson 4: Using Reinforcement Learning for Predictive Analytics

Question Number	Answer
1	strategy
2	True
3	rewards
4	False
5	3